HOW TO BUY & RESTORE
A COUNTRY HOME

HOW TO BUY & RESTORE
A COUNTRY HOME

JOANNA SIMMONS

COLLINS & BROWN

First published in Great Britain in 2006 by
Collins & Brown Ltd
Bramley Road
London W10 6SP

1 2 3 4 5 6 7 8 9

British Library Cataloguing-in-Publication Data:
A catalogue record for this title is available from
the British Library.

ISBN 1–84340–294-7

Reproduced by Anorax Limited
Printed in Singapore

CONTENTS

CHAPTER ONE

Life in the country

Many of us dream of moving to the countryside. It's a seductive fantasy. We'll leave the noisy, overcrowded city, with its unfriendly people and aggressive attitudes, for a clean-living, slower-paced life in a quiet rural backwater. We'll buy a postcard-pretty cottage, grow sweet peas in the garden and know the locals in the village pub.

This dream becomes a reality for some 115,000 people each year, who migrate from Britain's urban centres to rural districts, joining the 14 million who already live there. They leave for a multitude of reasons, but most have in common the quest for a better quality of life. Less pollution and stress, lower crime rates, a more gentle pace: these are the things that country life can offer. Then there are its unique attractions. Homes with real character and a garden. A safer environment for children, friendly neighbours and a sense of community. There is access to open spaces and with it a reconnection with the natural world and the seasons.

This chapter introduces the countryside to the urban dweller. There's information about what life in a rural environment is really like, from the highs of summer walks in the fields, to the lows of being cut off by snow in winter. There's the lowdown on what a rural property can offer – how running and living in a home in the country may be quite different from a property in the city. And there are case studies from individuals who have made the move and never regretted it, and from those who found that country living wasn't for them. It's all here to help make the transition from the big smoke to a quiet village as easy as possible. Do it right and you'll never look back.

What does 'country' mean?

The countryside across Britain is rich and varied, with the north, central Wales and Scotland less populated than the Midlands, south and southwest. From the type of landscape to the number of inhabitants, the weather conditions to the local architecture, there's a corner of Britain that's right for every ex-urbanite – you just need to know where to look.

In the middle of nowhere

If you really want to get away from it all, you can. Try Scotland and the Isles, central Wales, deepest Norfolk or around the Yorkshire Dales or North York Moors. Here, you will find remote houses, beautiful scenery and a rare feeling of isolation and stillness.

More than two million homes in Britain do not have mains gas. The more remote they are, the more certain it is that they won't be connected to mains supplies, which means relying on oil or LPG (liquefied petroleum gas) for heating and cooking. If you're deep into the wilds, you may not be connected to mains electricity and will need a generator. If you are connected to the national grid, heavy storms can mean power failure to your property and winter snows can cut you off. A car, preferably a 4x4, is essential. You could be a few miles away from a village with basic amenities and several hours' drive from a large town. Mobile phones don't work in some remoter parts of the country.

A hamlet

The dictionary definition of a hamlet is 'a small village, usually without a church'. Typically, it has just a handful of houses and few or no amenities. Life here is quiet, but at least there might be a friendly face up the road to borrow a cup of sugar from. You will probably feel marooned without a car – a hamlet is unlikely to be on a public transport route – but the seclusion and quiet are unique and soothing, and you are usually only a short drive or bike ride from a village with some facilities.

A village

Many villages started life as farms with surrounding buildings; others were community settlements, home bases for mixed farming communities whose residents all worked on the land or in related trades. Village populations have fluctuated over the centuries, notably when many residents left to find work in the cities during the industrial revolution of the 19th century. Since the increased urbanisation of that period, villages have come to occupy a more romanticised place in our collective imagination: not as working rural settlements, but as examples of quintessential Britain and honest rural life. When we think of England in particular, we usually imagine a sleepy village with a church, pub and green where cricket is played in summer. These are not the hard-working rural communities that Thomas Hardy wrote of, where life was decidedly unromantic, but a rarefied picture that is an antidote to the weary urban grind.

In the past 40 years, some villages have experienced mixed fortunes. Many went into decline in the seventies and eighties. The rise of the supermarket and prevalence of cars were the death knell for village shops and the closure of village schools robbed communities of much of their character. Today, though, many villages have been revitalised by the market for quality local shops selling regional produce and the overhaul of rural pubs, which now typically serve good food and local beers. Urban migrants have also been a positive influence in many villages, injecting money, energy and new business ideas into even the remotest settlements.

There tends to be some community spirit in all but the quietest villages, with anything from a parish council to a branch of the Women's Institute (WI), a tots' playgroup to yoga in the church hall. Remember, though, that commuter villages may not be so sociable, as everyone clears

out in the week to work and then collapses, exhausted, at the weekend. Before you move, do your research carefully. Ask around – local shopkeepers and the pub landlord will be able to tell you what the place is like on weekdays. Visit during the week and at weekends, too, to get a feel for how lively the village is.

A town

In terms of amenities, many rural towns offer everything you need, perhaps with the exception of a large supermarket. In its place, you'll increasingly find quality small shops selling local produce, offering a way of shopping that's more rewarding and sustaining to the local community. Towns have better public transport links to other major centres, plus extras like restaurants, banks, a doctor's surgery, a vet, maybe even a leisure centre or small cinema, providing plenty of life, on a small scale, deep in the country.

Life in a rural property – the gritty reality

Unless you move into a brand new home, you will probably find living in a rural property quite different from an urban one. Every house differs. How well it's been maintained by previous owners, its position (in a sheltered valley or high on a wind-blasted hill), layout and level of modernisation will all affect how comfortable or convenient it is to live in, but some generalisations can be made.

Older properties can be draughty, damp or difficult to heat. High ceilings, big rooms and ill-fitting doors and windows will challenge even the most efficient modern central heating system. To combat this and create real character, rural properties often have open fires. They not only look welcoming but can also create a great deal of heat. Many rural residents use a combination of central heating and open fires to warm their homes successfully, and often choose simply to keep one or two key rooms warm, rather than trying to keep the whole property at one temperature. You soon acclimatise to the cooler air of some parts of the house.

The property's layout will influence how warm it is, too. While a low-ceilinged cottage should, in theory, retain heat better than a grand Georgian rectory with high ceilings, the often linear layout of cottages, with rooms flowing into each other rather than opening off a central hall, can mean draughts circulate easily. Keeping doors shut and curtains drawn can alleviate this

problem. It's something you might not have had to consider in your thermally efficient, open-plan city home, but it's an easy detail to get used to.

You may find the very things that drew you to your new home are what make it harder to live in, but a willingness to accept some alterations in your lifestyle will go a long way to accommodating these changes. An inglenook fireplace may look wonderful, but come winter you may find that much of the heat roars straight up the chimney. Traditional sash or leaded light windows are charming, but if not well maintained can let in draughts. They are historic and characterful elements of your home, which are there to be enjoyed, but just remember that a period house may not function as efficiently as its modern neighbour.

Remember, too, that just because you don't like a feature of your rural property, it doesn't mean you can change it. If the property is listed, all of it – interior and exterior – is protected by law and Listed

Building Consent will be needed from the local planning authority for all but the most minor works of repair or maintenance.

Even if the building is not officially protected, think twice before you install modern 'improvements' like uPVC windows or fancy modern radiators – you could be destroying the very character that first attracted you.

Maintenance is a greater consideration – and responsibility – on a period rural property, too (we go into more detail on this subject later in the book). The exterior of a coastal house will take a beating from the strong sea winds and salt in the atmosphere, which can corrode paintwork, while any building in a wooded area will suffer from gutters clogged with leaves. These need regular clearing to ensure water drains away and doesn't leak into the fabric of the building, causing damp and rot. The extra work you take on with a rural home is, of course, offset by the beauty of the location, which most homeowners feel more than makes up for a little regular maintenance. Urban properties are on the whole easier to look after, but you need to be prepared to roll up your sleeves once in a while to keep your country home in good condition.

The structure and fabric of an old rural property may be quite different from an urban home. Materials like lime and hair plaster and distemper may have been used. The property may be timber framed, rather than the brick structures most city dwellers are familiar with. It may have clapboard cladding or tile-hung walls on its exterior, a thatched or slate roof. Interesting details like these require higher levels of maintenance and care than a modern bricks and mortar home. And when repairs are needed, you will have to source traditional materials and skilled tradesmen, both of which can cost more than a bog-standard builder using off-the-shelf materials.

In short, the larger the property and its garden, the more work you will have to do to keep it well maintained. There will also be jobs that you simply cannot manage yourself – repairing a thatch roof or lopping overhanging branches from a nearby tree – so you need to have the financial resources to look after your property and grounds correctly. But don't be put off. Invest a little time and money in your rural home and it will more than repay you in quality of life and a real sense of belonging.

Restoring a rented cottage

Lucie-Clare Watson, an interior designer, and her husband Oliver and 14-year-old son Charlie live in an 18th-century grade II listed stone cottage in the Peak District. They lease the property from a local estate and have substantially restored it since becoming tenants in 1992.

What work have you done?
We rewired, put on a new roof and redecorated extensively, stripping off the Artex, which was soaking because of damp. We used local builders who are used to working on this kind of listed property. Things like the guttering and downpipes all had to be reconditioned originals, but they understood that.

How much maintenance does the property need? Old houses are like the Forth Bridge – they always need work. The trick is to do something every year. If you did all your repairs and improvements 10 years ago, they will all need redoing at the same time 10 years later. Stagger the work, so you don't suddenly find yourself with mountains to do and a huge bill.

What's it like to live in a period property? Oliver and I like it, but we have an accepting attitude. Old houses are colder than new, there might be a bit of damp here and there, but it doesn't matter. As long as the place is well heated and ventilated, you won't have a problem. You have to accept that you live in an old house, that this is how people used to live. Light a fire every so often, keep the chimney in good shape and swept, and air the whole place whenever you can – that's the key.

Did you add any modern comforts?
We put in central heating. Some locals didn't agree with that, they said: 'Up here we just put another jumper on', but we fitted an oil-fired boiler.

Old properties are full of character, but need regular maintenance.

Living in the countryside – what to expect

Moving to the countryside means not only changing your locality, but also your whole approach to life – the most successful moves occur when this shift happens. You have to abandon old priorities and habits and develop new ones. It means changing your mental attitude from 'city thought' to 'rural think' and learning to understand the lives of long-term country dwellers, your new neighbours. Treat moving to the countryside as though you are moving to a foreign country and you're less likely to get caught out.

Here are some key issues to prepare for:

Accessibility

In all but the most vibrant villages, shopping, getting to work or school and visiting friends mean a car journey. Public transport will not necessarily be sufficient. You are also less likely to come across late-night stores, street lighting and takeaway deliveries. Cheap easy hops in a taxi from place to place are something only city dwellers enjoy.

Property prices

In the past, one of the chief attractions of moving to the countryside was the chance to snap up a chocolate-box cottage for a pittance or a whole estate for the same price as an urban semi. Not so today. Many areas carry property price tags to rival even the most desirable city residences. Devon and Cornwall, the Home Counties (from where London is still a commutable distance), East Anglia, Dorset and Yorkshire have all seen massive leaps in house prices, thanks to the urban exodus. Many parts of rural Wales are also rising fast – unsurprising when, according to one report, 40% of farm buildings sold in Wales in 2003 were bought by urban professionals. Across Wales, house prices rose by 16% in 2004, by just over 27% in the northwest and by almost 26% in the north, according to the Halifax Building Society. Improved rail transport and road networks, people's willingness to commute and technological advancements that make working from home a reality for all kinds of professions, have created a city exodus that's driving up rural property prices.

You can still find affordable property, of course, and maybe even the odd bargain. In the East Midlands, Yorkshire and Humberside, the north and northwest, house prices continue to climb, but the average cost of a house is still a great deal less than in the south. According to online estate agents Rightmove, it's just under £145,000 in Yorkshire and Humberside and just under £153,000 in the East Midlands (figures from January 2005).

If you are prepared to undertake restoration work, you may be able to create a unique and beautiful home for less than the cost of its restored neighbour. Be aware, though, that in some pockets of Britain – Devon, for example – most old farm buildings and run-down houses have already been developed, such is the interest in this approach to home ownership. You will also find property of great character in the countryside, built to local traditions with local materials and forming a key part of the surrounding architecture. Rural properties also tend to stay in the same hands longer than urban, so local neighbours can probably tell you much about former residents, giving you a special sense of history and place that is seldom found in the city.

The great outdoors

Living in the countryside means, of course, that you'll be closer to nature. Greater awareness of the seasons is a real bonus of country life. With a garden that comes in and out of flower, fields that are ploughed in winter then golden with wheat by autumn, and trees growing then dropping their leaves as spring moves to summer and autumn, you will be back in tune with the year's natural cycle.

Just as you are more aware of the seasons in a rural home, you are much more aware of the weather, too. Good weather in spring and summer will allow you to live much of your life outdoors – eating, relaxing, gardening and walking are all treats that can be enjoyed until late into the evening during the long, warm mid-summer days. Country residents are better able to make the most of good weather than the poor city dweller, who has only a crowded park to walk in on fine days. A garden, quiet lanes to wander in and an abundance of walking trails make it easy to be outside as soon as the sun is out. Many ex-urbanites spend less time commuting once they move to the countryside, too, where traffic jams are less frequent.

The flip side of this idyll is that British summers are notoriously short: lush meadows and blossoming gardens will become soggy, barren and muddy come winter – altogether less welcoming. When it's wet outside, you and your pets are more likely to tread mud into the house. Roads can become flooded and impassable and driving is often more challenging.

Heavy storms can cause more damage to an elderly house in a rural setting than an urban one, especially if it is bordered by trees that could fall, damaging tiles and chimneys and cutting off the power supply.

Snows can make driving impossible – the more remote and northerly you live, the more likely you are to be temporarily cut off by a downfall. Your picturesque home on the banks of a river may also be prone to flooding in winter – check the Environment Agency's Flood Map before you buy, to see if the area is at risk.

A word about winter, too… Winter days are short and, without the lights and liveliness of a city to distract you, this will become far more apparent. When you're living far from amenities like shops, cinemas and restaurants, it's easy to feel claustrophobic in your house as yet another gloomy winter day fades away. But while this may sound unappealing, many rural properties come into their own at this time of year, offering levels of cosiness that urban homes seldom do. Open fires, an Aga perhaps, low ceilings and a real sense of shutting out the wild weather when you return home are extremely comforting. That gratifying feeling of returning to the warmth after a bracing walk or a chilly afternoon in the garden is palpable and thrilling. You cherish and enjoy the indoors far more during a winter in the countryside.

The garden

A larger garden than you might be able to have in the city is a draw for many ex-urbanites, offering you the chance to develop a gardening passion and perhaps grow your own fruit and vegetables. A terrace or deck area serves as an outside room, too, adding a real sense of space to your home and allowing you to spill outdoors whenever the weather is fine.

Dreams of summer barbecues, flower-filled borders and rolling lawns are naturally persuasive, but remember the amount of work a sizeable garden needs. Do you have the time to maintain a large garden? Do you have the right equipment and expertise to cope with it? You will need a good mower, a strong hedge trimmer, maybe even a chainsaw, or you will need the financial resources to pay someone to keep on top of basics like mowing, weeding and hedge trimming. You may also come across the kinds of problems city gardeners never encounter. Deer eating all your carefully grown flowers, for example, or the local cattle breaking through your fences to get at your lawn.

Meeting people

Even the smallest communities can be lively, sociable places to live. Rural life, in all but the most remote corners, is generally less anonymous and private than in cities. Neighbours can become friends, willing to help out, the local shopkeeper, postman and landlord are familiar village faces that everyone knows, and there's a more relaxed, open atmosphere. Of course, you must be prepared to integrate. Marching into the local pub in a city-sharp suit and ordering champagne might ruffle feathers, particularly in Britain's more remote pockets. Don't try to replicate your city life in the countryside, or expect people to share all your interests. Make an effort and find some common ground. Join local societies, use the pub and village stores (if they exist), introduce yourself and ask neighbours for advice on any local or domestic matters. Most importantly, be patient. Friendships take time to become established, wherever you live.

Young children are often quicker to make friends and adapt to a new lifestyle than adults. For them, the countryside can be one huge playground, with space to ride their bikes, explore, build dens and generally tear around. Crime rates are lower in the countryside and most parents feel it is a safer environment in which to raise children, allowing them freedoms they cannot have in the city. Nevertheless, it can be a mistake to assume that children will automatically and easily slot into their new rural life. Expect them to have their own struggles with the adjustment and give them time to settle in. While the countryside can prove a glorious environment for play and exploration for young children, for teenagers country life can be boring and isolated. With friends scattered far and wide and poor public transport, they rely heavily on parents to shuttle them around until old enough to drive themselves, which can be a strain for everyone. Living close to a large secondary school will at least guarantee that other teenagers also live nearby. A leisure centre, cinema or active youth club in the area is also a major plus. And before you make any decision to move, talk at length to your teenage offspring about their needs and preferences, involve them at each stage of house buying if at all possible and be prepared to compromise until you find a new rural home that suits all members of the family.

Next page: The countryside's open spaces are a giant playground for children.

Are you suited to life in the country?

Property quiz

Before you splash out on a waxed jacket and wellies, try this quiz to see how well you would manage living in the countryside.

Your past experience of country life is…

a) You grew up in the countryside and now, after years of city life, want to get back to it.

b) You were brought up on the edge of a large town, but loved having access to the countryside.

c) You are city born and bred and have spent only a few weeks on holiday in a rural environment.

Your friends and family are…

a) All in the area you're hoping to move to. That's why you're moving there.

b) Some are quite a distance from where you hope to move, but your parents will be close by and you hope other friends visit because you will miss them.

c) All in one city. And too exhausted/work-stressed/busy seeing each other to leave it at the weekends.

When it comes to grocery shopping…

a) You're very organised and buy everything you need in one weekly shop.

b) You like to buy fresh things each day on your way back from work, but stock up once a week in a supermarket on basics.

c) You eat out a lot and, when at home, order takeaways.

Travel…

a) You drive everywhere and are used to covering distances on dark roads.

b) You drive, but your teenage children don't. They will want to go out with friends and that could mean a lot of late night ferrying.

c) You use buses and trains. After a night out, you just hop in a taxi.

How do you cope with chilly days?

a) You don't feel the cold, and prefer fresh air and warm clothes to an overheated house.

b) You don't like your house to be sweltering, but do enjoy being able to heat it up quickly by just turning up the thermostat.

c) You like wandering round the house in a T-shirt in winter, heating cranked up full.

Some tiles have slipped off your roof and the local authority conservation officer insists you replace them with traditionally made replicas that are twice as expensive as modern versions.

a) No problem. You want to restore your house in the most sympathetic way possible.

b) You don't have enough money to fund the repairs for now. They will have to wait.

c) Forget that. You're irritated that the job now needs more money and research time spent on it. You'll get a cowboy to fix cheap modern tiles and hope the conservation officer doesn't penalise you for it.

Kitten heels and country walks don't go together. Will you mind?

a) No. You're happiest in flat shoes or wellies and jeans. Clothes are about practicality not fashion.

b) Not much. You're no slave to fashion, but do take an interest. Traipsing around in muddy wellies might pall after a while, but if there's a city nearby where you can have a glamorous night out, you'll be fine.

c) Yes. You're used to dressing smartly for work and play; hard, dry pavements and carpeted office floors to walk on; and taxis to whisk you home at the first sign of rain.

Winter days are short and dark – will you find this a problem?

a) You don't suffer from SAD (seasonal affective disorder) and the chance to reconnect with the seasons appeals.

b) You plan to work from home, so those short days could leave you feeling rather isolated and claustrophobic. Hopefully, a roaring open fire will compensate.

c) You like the 24-hour buzz of big cities, which helps to keep winter's worst at bay. Oh, and you hate driving at night.

Answers

If you answered predominantly As, you already have a good understanding of country living and should integrate well with the rural community.

If you answered mostly Bs, be prepared to make some adjustments for rural life, but don't give up on the dream of moving.

If you answered mostly Cs, perhaps town life really does suit you best. Are you sure you want to move out?

Leaving the city

Tessa Williams, a freelance journalist, and husband Peter Elliott, a firefighter, sold their north London home and moved to a village in Northants in January 2002. They bought a four-bedroom Victorian end-of-terrace cottage with a huge garden looking out over fields for their children, Joe (nine) and Beth (five), to play in.

Why move to the countryside?
Pete and I were fed up with our small two-up two-down. It had suited us fine as a couple, but with two children it was tiny and there was no storage. We looked in London, but couldn't afford to move to a nice area.

What have been the key advantages?
We got masses more for our money than we would have done back in the capital – double the space inside and lots of green space outside, plus a slower pace of life and new friends. We have more time and are not commuting in horrendous traffic.

Was it easy to make new friends?
Quite difficult at first. I think people are more reserved in a village. You have to be careful, because you are stuck with each other, so residents choose their friends carefully. But the more you live here, the more you find that a lot of people are in exactly the same position as you. Not everyone who lives in the country is from a farming background.

How have you had to adapt? A bigger house and garden involves a lot more upkeep. We ended up getting a cleaner. I'd never looked after a big place and two kids before. I'd never done any gardening, either, and our back garden is big. Coming from a city, that's been quite overwhelming, but I've loved learning all about it.

Any tips? For me, it was important to be near a big city. The village is a one-shop place, but it's a five-minute drive to Northampton, where the kids can still go to McDonalds and I can go to Sainsburys. It helped soften the transition from city life to country.

Was it a good move? Yes. Pete and I are less stressed. There is lots of open space nearby and summer is lovely. The children are very happy. I'm glad for all our sakes that we moved.

Opposite: A move to the countryside usually means the opportunity to own a larger house with access to open green space.

How will you earn a living?

Unless you're hoping to try a Tom and Barbara style self-sufficiency experiment, you will still need to work to survive in the countryside. Some people move because their jobs relocate them, but more move because their jobs will allow them to relocate. Few people move to the countryside actually to work in it. But if you have a profession or trade that's in demand anywhere in the UK – a teacher, plumber or nurse, say – then it's easier to make the leap.

Another possibility is to work some or all of the time from home, a solution many city-based organisations are increasingly open to. It means commuting for some of the week or month, but can be a satisfying option for employer and employee. You are still a presence in the office and can attend meetings, but you are not chained to a Monday to Friday commute that can be draining, both physically and financially.

Working remotely relies on adequate phone and internet connections. BT broadband connection is now available for the whole country as long as you are within 6–10km of a BT exchange and have a BT phone point. If you do need additional phone lines installed at your house, try to make sure you get them put in during the initial building stage (if there is one), so that sockets and cabling cause least disruption to the house's fabric.

If you are considering staying in your same city job, make sure you have investigated the commute properly. Find out train times (what if you had to work late?), the price of a season ticket and, if applicable, how much more it costs to park your car at the station. If you can, try the journey a few times to get a feel for how crowded the train becomes. Talk to fellow commuters to find out how often the train is delayed. If your journey into work would involve driving, try it out a few times during rush hour and don't forget to factor petrol and parking costs into your moving plans.

Moving to the countryside need not mean a longer commute – many people switch to working from home full or part time and enjoy views like this from their office.

CHAPTER TWO

How to buy

This chapter covers the practicalities of finding and buying a new home. There is detailed information on all the ways to track down and buy your dream rural property, from private sales to auctions. Not everyone who relocates to the countryside finds their new home by simply walking into an estate agent. There are plenty of other ways to search out the perfect property. Estate agents are an obvious first port of call, but many specialist agencies and societies also advertise properties for sale around Britain, including Save Britain's Heritage and the Society for the Protection of Ancient Buildings (SPAB).

There are tips on how to tackle the logistics of the move: how to cope if the area you plan to move to is miles from your current home; what sort of time scale to factor in for a long distance relocation; and the possible methods you can adopt to make selling in the city and buying in the country easier. We also take a look at what relocation agencies can offer, outline how the house purchasing system operates in Scotland and examine whether renting before you buy is a good idea.

Tracking down a dream property

Finding your perfect home in the countryside takes perseverance and time, and there are a number of ways to do it. Here are some places to start. (See chapter 9 for full contact details of organisations and agents.)

- Outside, walk around the boundary and notice how close neighbours are. In summer, this could mean noise or lack of privacy. Check any outbuildings for their condition and current usage.

- Rural estate agents. If you know the area you want to move to, build up a relationship with the agents there: they'll have good local knowledge. Don't wait for them to call – phone regularly to see what's coming onto the market. Let them know what's happening with the sale of your home, too. Being a cash buyer or having no chain makes you instantly more appealing to an estate agent in search of a straightforward and speedy sale.

- Regional estate agents with specialist knowledge. If you know exactly what type of property you want to buy, you may find that a larger regional estate agent, with branches across a wide area, has an office dedicated to that type of home. For example, southwest estate agents Stags has a Waterside office, dealing exclusively with homes on or

overlooking the coast and rivers of Devon, Cornwall and Somerset.

- The internet. Most estate agents now have websites, although some are more efficient at updating theirs than others. Even so, the internet is an excellent place to gather estate agent details in a number of areas, all from the comfort of your home.

- The Property Organisation and Pavilions of Splendour are agents specialising in listed buildings and those of architectural or historical interest, many in need of work. Pavilions of Splendour's website also has a central register of listed properties for sale throughout Britain, many through private vendors.

- Period Property UK has a website where you can buy and sell period property.

- The Society for the Protection of Ancient Buildings (SPAB) issues a quarterly booklet of buildings of historical interest in need of repair and for sale in Britain to its members. In the past, it has sold properties as diverse as a Victorian pumping station in Cambridgeshire and an old lookout tower in the Highlands (with plenty of cottages and timber-framed farmhouses in between). SPAB membership is £30 per year for an individual, £45 joint membership or £500 for life.

🐦 Save Britain's Heritage (SAVE) compiles an annual Buildings At Risk register that highlights historic buildings that are vacant with the aim of finding new owners able to repair them or find new uses for them. Most are listed. It costs £12, or you can access the larger online catalogue by subscribing to the website at £15 for 12 months.

🐦 The church occasionally sells off property in need of conversion or repair. In Scotland, contact the Church of Scotland's law department – its website of property for sale is updated weekly; in England and Wales, individual dioceses often have a property services office, although calling each one would be time

consuming. Many old churches and chapels end up in the SPAB's booklet (see above), so check that first.

🐦 Damaged or dilapidated properties sometimes fall into the possession of local councils (particularly old commercial or religious buildings). Call your local Regeneration and Development department.

🐦 Private sales. Home owners sometimes sell their property privately, which avoids paying costly estate agents' fees. This may sometimes be reflected in the sale price – a plus for the buyer. If you buy this way, you will be dealing directly with the seller, which means avoiding potential estate agency hard sell, and it can prove a faster and more efficient way to buy. National and local newspapers carry adverts in their classified or property sections, although private sales often rely on word of mouth – not so helpful when you're house hunting in Derbyshire but still living in London. The internet can help. Sites like www.buyitprivately.com detail thousands of properties for sale privately across Britain.

Buying at auction

Buying a house at auction is becoming more and more popular. In 2003, more than 30,000 properties – 8% of the all properties sold in Britain – were sold at auction. So what makes it such an appealing way to buy?

One of the key advantages is speed. Buying a house in the traditional way can be long-winded and often jeopardised by complicated chains: almost a third of all agreed sales fall through. By contrast, the auction process is quick and efficient.

Another attraction is the dream of finding your perfect property at a fraction of the market value – not necessarily just an idle fancy. Prices are often significantly cheaper than those you see in estate agents' windows. The only caveat to this is that the sale price depends entirely on how many other would-be buyers are bidding for your dream home. It's very easy for a bidding war to start.

There's a wider choice of location, too. Auctions, wherever they are being held, can contain properties from all over the country, which makes them ideal hunting grounds for a city dweller looking to move to the countryside, but flexible about exactly where. There tends to be a bigger variety of property, too, with unique places that are difficult to value, repossessed homes needing a quick sale and any unusual property that might be difficult to sell through normal channels, all coming under the auctioneer's hammer.

Buying at auction is a completely transparent process: an open and fair competition between bidders. You cannot be gazumped, or the sale go to sealed bids as with traditional methods, because once the auctioneer's gavel falls, the sale is complete and binding. The time scale involved is remarkably quick, too. Once sold, the property is yours and the completion date is fixed in advance – usually 28 days after the sale.

How to prepare for an auction

A property auction isn't something to wander into on a whim. You should be well prepared. Here are five key steps to getting ready for auction day.

1   Get hold of the auction catalogue well in advance so that you have time to look at any property. To find out when and where auctions are taking place, check the local press, ask estate agents or call the Royal Institute of Chartered Surveyors (RICS) Contact Centre for local auctions. Its website has a list of auctioneers, too.

2   Once you've viewed the property, instruct a surveyor to visit and write a

report; you'll need this at least one week before the sale. It may suggest further specialist reports or enquiries to be made, and can give an idea of repair costs.

3 Instruct your solicitor to inspect local and national searches and the title deeds for any onerous covenants or restrictions, just as you would with any conventional property purchase. He/she should also check with local authorities about any other factors that might affect the property, like new roads or redevelopment. Once you've done all that and everything seems satisfactory, then – and only then – are you ready to bid.

3 Work out an upper limit you're prepared to spend, based on the survey and projected cost of work. Don't get carried away and swept into a bidding war. Remember this figure and stick to it. Factor in stamp duty, solicitor's and surveyor's charges, as well as the auctioneer's fee.

5 Before the auction, find out how and what you'll be expected to pay if you're the successful bidder. Typically, the auction house requires a 10% deposit immediately after the sale, so you'll need funds ready, and you must be in a position to pay the remainder within 28 days.

And remember…

- Properties can sometimes sell prior to auction. Check with the auctioneer to confirm that the lot in which you are interested is still being offered.

- Never bid for a property at auction if your purchase depends on selling your own house.

- Be aware that on signing the contract you'll be responsible for insuring the building.

Other ways to buy – I wonder who owns that?

We have all experienced those times when, wandering through a quiet village or across a field, you spy the tumbledown cottage or shabby farmhouse of your dreams. If you really lose your heart to it, how can you make it yours?

If the property is inhabited…

- You could knock on the door and ask about ownership. It takes courage, but you *might* be lucky. Perhaps the owner is thinking of moving, or has just inherited it from an elderly relative and is keen to sell?

- Leafleting properties, asking whether the owners wish to sell and suggesting a private sale, is also occasionally successful. Write a letter explaining what you're looking for and why you're interested in that area.

If the property is empty…

- Contact the conservation officer at the local council to check what, if anything, is known about the owner.

- Check the electoral roll, council tax and even probate records through your local council records office.

- Ask around – in the pub or at the post office.

- Look at the Land Registry website, where you can download title information for a £2 fee.

- Alternatively, pay an agency to research the property's ownership for you. 1stlocate charges £100 for properties or land in England and Wales: in Scotland, it's £30.

The problem, particularly in rural areas where properties have remained in the same family for generations and often as part of a large estate, is that an estimated third of Britain's 18 million properties aren't registered with the Land Registry, or the title is unclear. In England and Wales, registration has only recently been made compulsory, but even then the rules apply only when a property changes hands. In Scotland, all land and property has been recorded in the Register of Sasines since 1617, but it is sometimes unreliable as entries are only now being transferred to the state-guaranteed Land Register.

If you fall in love with a country cottage, ask the owner if they're considering moving – you might strike lucky.

Using a property finder

If you have no time to find a house yourself, you can pay an agency to do it for you. Called anything from relocation agents to home-search or property-acquisition agents, they are part of a private home-search industry that is thriving. Some companies operate on a nationwide basis; some cover large areas, taking in four or five counties; others cater to more specific needs, for example, home finding for people who specifically wish to move from London to Hertfordshire.

What do they do?

They will take a detailed brief from you, the client, noting every aspect of the property you are looking for, including size, location, proximity to amenities or schools and, of course, price. They will then search for properties using a number of channels – estate agents, the internet, direct contacts and local networking. Once they have a long list of potential houses, they will visit a selection of properties to ascertain their suitability, create a short list of a select few (often between five and 10) and arrange a viewing itinerary for you, usually over two days. Once you have chosen a house, the agent handles all the negotiations and, with your agreement, makes the final offer.

The advantages of using property-acquisition agents

Their in-depth knowledge of an area enables them to match you with the town or village that best fulfils your needs. For example, if a good local school is one of your priorities, this will influence their search.

Agents will often find properties that you would not have been able to locate on your own, perhaps because they were not on the open market or because they were being privately or confidentially marketed. (Home owners keen to sell privately and save on estate agents' fees regularly contact property-acquisition agents.) The agents will also sometimes target homes not currently on the market via direct mailings.

Agents can often agree a lower purchase price than you would have achieved alone, thanks to their local property market knowledge and professional representation. This can save you a significant amount of money.

They also save you time. You don't have to call estate agents, sort through particulars and arrange viewings. Most home-finding agents also promise to find and complete purchase of your new home within three to six months.

By arranging familiarisation tours for you of an area you are interested in – by car or even helicopter – agents can save you effort.

Travelling to view properties in a new location that turns out to be unsuitable can be a huge source of frustration when buying independently, especially if you've had to travel a long distance.

Home-finding agents are not estate agents trying to push property. They sit on the other side of the desk, acting for you. They are respected by estate agents, who tend to treat enquiries from professional property-search consultants more seriously than enquiries from private buyers. This means they are often the first to hear of new properties entering the market. Buyers using a property-acquisition service are seen as preferred bidders in competitive situations.

Costs

Most property-acquisition agents charge an initial registration fee, typically around £500. In addition, they will take a percentage of the purchase price, often around 1%. Some take a further percentage of any saving between the asking price and the eventual purchase price they negotiated on your behalf, for any property you exchange contracts on. This is often around 15%.

How to buy in Scotland

The house-buying process in Scotland differs in several key ways from that in England and Wales. This brief explanation of the system outlines what to expect if you are buying north of the border.

The first difference is that most properties are sold through solicitors rather than estate agents, although estate agencies are becoming more commonplace. Solicitors in Scotland call themselves Solicitors and Estate Agents, and some set up Solicitors' Property Centres where details of all property for sale through solicitors in one area are advertised. Some solicitors' firms simply have their own property department with staff who deal with the non-legal aspects of buying and selling.

Solicitors

You must use a Scottish solicitor when buying a property in Scotland. Make sure the firm is a member of the Law Society of Scotland. It is best to find a solicitor before you make a formal offer on a property because of the complexity and binding nature of certain contracts under Scottish law.

Noting an interest

If you are interested in a property you have viewed, even if you are not ready to make an offer on it, you should register your interest with the seller's solicitor or estate agent. You don't have to have a solicitor yourself to do this, although one would be happy to undertake notification for you. This does not commit you to buy. It ensures that you will be kept informed of any progress in the house's sale.

Surveys

In Scotland, you get a survey done on the property before you make an offer, then make your offer based on its findings. Your solicitor will read the survey, too, and advise you about how much to offer. He will also confirm the existence of building warrants (often needed to alter or improve a building and issued by the local authority), planning permissions and completion certificates relating to any alterations to the building in the past.

Offers

Rather than having a fixed asking price, in Scotland most houses are advertised for sale at 'offers over £x' to encourage higher bids. However, if you can't afford the price, you can still make a lower offer. Properties are often sold at less than the 'offers over' price and, the longer the property has been on the market, the cheaper you are likely to get it. The 'offers over' price is simply the point at which bargaining starts.

Equally, you may have to offer above the price to secure a property. How big an extra percentage you should offer will depend on the area, type of property and state of the housing market. Your solicitor should be able to advise you.

An increasing number of properties are now being advertised for sale at a fixed price, similar to the system in England and Wales. Between 2003 and 2004 the number of fixed-price properties advertised in Edinburgh increased by 70%. This is partly because people from outside Scotland are put off by the 'offers over' system and also because it can make buying difficult. In England and Wales you would normally get a survey done on a property after you make an offer; in the Scottish system, if you find yourself outbid on a series of properties, having paid for a survey on each one, it can be an expensive process.

Closing dates for offers

If the house has had lots of interest from buyers, the vendor might decide to advise all those who have noted their interest that a closing date for offers has been set. This is designed to hurry the process along and set up a kind of blind auction where you and all other prospective buyers must make an offer by a set date. Unless you absolutely love the house, you should offer only what you think it is worth, not the amount you think might beat all other offers.

If you anticipate that a closing date for offers on a property might be set in the near future, you can still hurry the process along yourself by making an offer first. This is a way of shifting the pressure from purchaser to vendor. You may even be able to negotiate with the seller that you will pay a premium on your offer if they agree to sell it to you without going to a closing date.

Sellers are not obliged to accept the highest offer they receive after the closing date: they may be prepared to accept a lower offer where, for instance, the buyer is not dependent on selling his or her own property and can move quickly.

When your offer is accepted

Acceptance of your offer creates a legally binding contract and you will be provided with a copy of the formal offer for future reference. However, your offer can be made subject to certain conditions and, if these conditions are not agreed or met by the seller, you are no longer committed to the sale.

The practicalities of a long-distance move

Once you have decided to move to the countryside, worked out which area and even which type of house suits you and your family, you then need to consider the logistics involved.

Conducting viewings

There is no easy way to cope with the time-consuming process of looking at houses. If you are very lucky you might spot the perfect home in one viewing, but typically it takes around 14 viewings to find the property you end up buying.

If you are moving several hours' drive away, you can choose to arrange viewings at weekends. Many rural estate agents don't open on Sundays, so this means an early start every Saturday morning, a busy day looking at properties and then a drive home at the end of it. This way, you don't need to take time off work or spend money on overnight accommodation to house hunt.

The disadvantages? It's hard work and viewing a lot of properties in one day can be tiring and confusing. You run the risk of missing your dream home because you viewed it at the end of a packed day and were too jaded to take in its charms. You are also dependent on being able to arrange all your viewings on a

Saturday and must hope that none gets cancelled when you are already halfway up the motorway.

The alternative is to score through some days in your diary and use an extended period of time to search. Unless you have friends in the area, you will need to book a B&B or hotel. If you have small children, you will probably need to find someone to look after them: kids plus estate agents plus endless house viewings equals stress for everyone. The advantage of this method is that you will get to know the market, the local estate agents and what the area feels like to live in. You will also be in a position to zoom round to viewings as soon as properties come on the market. If you are house hunting miles from home, it's the only way to save wasting a lot of time and money on travel.

How fast can you sell your house?

It's no good finding a dream property and then losing it because your urban home takes months to sell. Then again, selling your current home in a week and finding that you are out on the street isn't ideal either. According to online estate agency Rightmove, the length of time properties spend on the market is rising, from 53 days during the summer of 2004 when the market was buoyant, to an average 87 days by January 2005. Take advice from local estate agents about how the market is moving in the area you live in and in the area you hope to move to. It might influence how soon you put your home on the market and whether you need to accept offers on it immediately or can hold out for the asking price.

When it comes to buying, even if you make an asking-price offer, some vendors won't agree to take their property off the market until you have a buyer for yours. Once you do have a buyer for your home and an offer accepted on the one you wish to buy, the conveyancing process in Britain typically takes at least three months, often longer.

Could you sell first?

If you have family or friends in the area you are moving to, you could sell your home first, put your furniture in storage and stay with them while you house hunt. This gives you the advantage of being a chain-free buyer – someone all vendors and estate agents love – and automatically puts you at the top of the buyers pile.

Could you rent first?

Another solution is to rent first. Renting a house in the area you're interested in for six months allows you to 'try it out' without committing. To cover yourself further, you could also rent out your urban home, so if you really don't take to country life, you have a place in the city to return to.

Renting also means that house hunting is more straightforward, as you are in situ. You can begin to get other areas of life sorted – finding work, registering with local services, settling children into school – before finding a house. Moving house is said to be one of life's most stressful experiences, so this approach spreads the load and allows you to make key lifestyle adjustments first.

CHAPTER THREE

What to look for

Buying a house is the biggest investment most of us make in our lives, and the suitability of our home is crucial to our well-being and happiness, so take each viewing seriously. There is more to looking round a house than checking the number of bedrooms and seeing if you like its atmosphere.

It's invaluable to have some understanding of how the building was put together, especially when buying an old property. This helps you to identify any danger signs and assess how complicated it will be to remedy them. A surveyor, architect or architectural historian may be able to accompany you on a second viewing to assess the health of the building.

You should also have a list of questions concerning the land the property stands on. Ownership, access rights and accessibility in winter are all relevant. And if you love the property but would like to change it – by extending a room – you need to know who would have authority over your plans. You also need to think beyond the house's boundary lines and consider whether it has the right amenities close by. Are there schools, a doctor and vet, or a reliable public transport network?

Finally, have a good idea of what properties are selling for and do not expect to find a bargain just because you are moving to the countryside. Victorian and Edwardian properties are popular because they are generally structurally sound and don't present enormous challenges. Older properties may require more complex work, but you're buying a piece of history, so they are rarely inexpensive.

Love at first sight

Ask yourself four general questions

1 Will the house work for me and my family? Don't buy an old building unless you are prepared to accept its particular character, warts and all. You should adapt to it, not the other way round. You may not be able to change the house's layout or extend it.

2 Is it reasonably sound? Get adequate surveys (see below) so you won't be caught out by unexpected problems that you cannot afford to tackle.

3 Do I love it? You need to feel passionately about the house – taking on a rural property, especially one that needs renovation, can be physically and financially draining.

4 Is it in the right area? Location is as important as the property itself.

Now for a closer inspection…

Before you call in the experts, perform your own lay person's survey to get a feel for potential problems.

Outside

Start at the top with the roof. Take along binoculars to look closely. Slight warping or unevenness on the surface of an old roof does not always indicate a structural problem, but it may mean the rafters within have bowed.

- How does the roof look? In a thatched property, damaged or rotted thatch can be replaced with overlays and patch repairs – it's not always necessary to dismantle and recover the whole roof.

- On slate roofs, minor cracks or flaking do not necessarily indicate that the roof needs replacing. Although slate roofing is a skilled job, replacing the odd missing or broken slate can be done by an amateur.

- Inspect the outside of the chimney. A leaning or cracked stack may not be dangerous, but you should get professional advice.

- Is there vegetation growing out of gutters and drainpipes? Visit on a wet day – are they leaking? Stand next to drainpipes and listen – is water flowing down? No special skills are required to unblock gutters and downpipes, but unless this is done they can send water into the brickwork without anyone noticing, causing damp or damaging mortar.

- Are there climbing plants on the walls? They can both create and conceal problems. Aggressive climbers like ivy can force rainwater pipes off walls and crack them, letting water soak undetected into the masonry.

- Can you see any cracks in the exterior render? These allow moisture to seep into the building, resulting in the render being forced off the wall during a frost. Tap the wall near any obvious damage: a hollow sound tells you that the render is loose and will need patching and consolidating.

- Where does the house lie? If the ground around it is higher, this can cause damp. Soil levels should always be below the internal floor level.

Inside

- Go upstairs. Look for leaks – dark patches on the ceilings and walls – which may mean an unsound roof or broken gutters.

- Downstairs, check for rising damp. Can you smell it? Are there dark marks above the skirting or damp course? Do the walls feel wet? Rising damp cannot

be left untreated and can be costly to eradicate.

- Look at the ceilings. Upstairs ceilings are generally attached directly to the roof timbers, so cracks in the plaster may indicate problems with the roof structure. Other ceilings are generally part of the floor above. Cracks will appear if the floor joists are overstressed, because of a particularly heavy piece of furniture above, for example. But cracks don't always signal major problems and in many cases there is no need to replace a whole ceiling, even those that are noticeably cracked and loose.

Causes for concern

Outside

- Cracks in the exterior that travel from inside to out, follow mortar joints or – obviously – are large enough to see daylight through, suggest movement in the building, which can be expensive to correct. Get a qualified structural engineer to look at them.

- Bowing brick walls: all bricks walls are susceptible to bowing, especially in Georgian properties where walls had little bonding and can split apart, but they can be tied together and restrained quite easily. A slightly bulging brick wall may be perfectly stable, but it

might be a sign of movement in the property, a far more serious problem. Seek advice from a structural engineer.

🦆 In a timber-framed house, do the bases of walls or posts bulge? This can indicate that they are soaking up water. Look at joints in the frame, too, if you can see them. They may be under pressure from carrying too much weight if a new wall has been built over them, or they may be deteriorating from centuries of exposure to the weather.

Inside

🦆 Are there cracks in the interior walls? Some cracks are historic, some are seasonal, caused by movement in clay soil as it absorbs moisture or dries out, but others are less superficial. If there are cracks in a partition wall, for example, seek advice from a professional (and not just from a builder). Some timber partition walls are load bearing and contain important bracing elements that can fail if the wall has been tampered with.

🦆 Is plaster falling off the walls? This can sometimes be consolidated with grout, but may need replacing.

Historic buildings like this need special attention, but the pleasure that can be gained from living in such a place is enormous.

🦆 Is the ceiling lath and plaster? If it is falling down, it may be possible to repair it with screw fixings, but often total renewal is needed.

🦆 In the roof space, can you seen signs of dry rot fungi, wet rot or insect attack? Look for actual fungi or white root-like threads called mycelium that can indicate dry rot; soft, spongy wet timber may mean wet rot; while flaking timber with bore holes and fallen dust is a sign of insect attack, past or present. All will need attention from a specialist.

Check for damp, cracks and rot inside when you view an old rural property.

Behind the façade

Check this list of problems that are not always obvious when viewing any property and be prepared to ask plenty of questions.

Is the house connected to basic services: gas, electricity and water? If not, could they be installed easily?

What's the sewerage or waste system? If the property has a septic tank, how old is it? Older tanks are often damaged or may be too small to cope with the quantity of water a modern household uses.

Is access a problem? Is the property down an unmade road that would be inaccessible to lorries? Does it become impassable in winter? This could be crucial if you're planning work that requires deliveries.

What is your right of access? You may need to cross someone else's land to get to yours. Check the owner is happy for delivery lorries to use the route and that you are within your rights to cross the land.

Are there trees growing close to the house? If the property is in a conservation area or is listed, you must apply to lop or fell trees. This could also affect plans to extend the property.

Are there outhouses or buildings? If the main house is a listed building, it's likely that any outhouses or other buildings are, too, and protected by the same restrictions.

Who owns the bordering land? Contact the Land Registry to see if it is registered. If the land is unregistered, you could consult the electoral register to see who the last owner was and try to trace the current owner from them. Ask your local planning department whether any proposals for development have been applied for and what their policy would be should such a request come up.

Are there any public paths crossing your land? Estate agents' details should make this clear. Consult the Definitive Map at your local planning department that shows rights of ways for walkers, riders and vehicles. If someone has used a path in the past 20 years, it is officially a public footpath and hiking groups like the Ramblers Association may apply for old paths to be revived, which could be intrusive. Be especially wary of bridle paths, as they are often used by motorbikes.

What to look out for in ancient buildings

Timber-framed buildings

Some distortion of old timber is not generally a sign of weakness, but of natural movement while the timber was still 'green' (unseasoned timber was commonly used in the past). Where failure in heavy timber framing does occur, it tends to do so at the joints. They may need replacing – a structural engineer can advise.

The walls of timber-framed buildings were usually made wind- and water-tight with infill panels of wattle and daub. These were woven from oak staves and hazel withies, then covered with daub – a mix of sand, clay and cow dung, with chopped animal hair or straw added to reinforce it. Where these panels still exist, every effort should be made to preserve them, which is a specialist job, as they are an important part of the fabric.

Thatched homes

Thatch is a good insulator and adds enormous character to a house, but its life span is shorter than that of slate, clay or stone tiles. Thatch is affected by climatic conditions – very damp surroundings or wet weather will hasten its demise. In parts of Devon, high humidity shortens the life expectancy of thatch, while parts of East Anglia benefit from the drying effect of North Sea winds. Roof camber is also crucial. The roof needs a steep angle of 50 degrees so that the thatch can shed rainwater effectively. Strong winds can damage thatch, as can animals, typically squirrels and rats.

The most common types of thatch are water reed, which lasts 55–65 years (and is the most expensive); combed wheat, with a life span of 20–40 years; and long straw (prevalent in East Anglia), which lasts 15–25 years. Even if the thatch looks in a poor state, it's not always necessary to replace it: patch repairs and overlays can often be added and soon blend in.

Contrary to popular belief, thatched roofs pose no greater fire risk than tiled roofs, although sensible owners will take steps to ensure their house is well protected. To minimise risk, electrical wiring in the roof space should be checked by an electrician. Chimney stacks should be inspected for thin walls or holes through which hot gas can leak and eventually ignite, setting fire to the thatch. Be careful to keep the roof space clear of old thatch or straw dust.

If you are thinking of buying a thatched home, get a thorough survey done on the roof. This will give an idea of the work needed in years to come, which is useful when you consider that thatchers are often booked up for years in advance.

If you own a thatched house, you should take out specialist insurance, which is not as expensive as you might think. Specialists include NFU Mutual and County Insurance Services. Grants are also sometimes available for repair. Check with your local authority.

The Thatching Advisory Services website has advice on surveys, insurance, finding a thatcher and all other issues related to owning or buying a thatched house.

Properties by the sea

Strong winds and corrosive salt in the air mean the exterior of a coastal property needs more maintenance than its inland equivalent. Battering storms and high winds can dislodge TV aerials and rip off tiles. The brine in the air will corrode paintwork, causing it to bubble and flake much faster than on sheltered properties. Any cast or wrought ironwork – fences, railing – will need a regular coat of paint, with rust carefully cleaned off first.

Flooding is also an issue in heavy storms. Climate change has meant severe storms

Thatch adds enormous character to a home and can last for up to 65 years.

are now more common and many sea defences no longer provide adequate protection. There is also a small risk of coastal erosion affecting properties by cliffs. Some homes on the Yorkshire coast have seen their gardens reduce in size dramatically over the years.

Properties by a river

According to the Environment Agency, five million homes across the country are at risk of flooding and that figure is set to rise. Damage to a property from even a minor flood can be extensive and it takes time to dry out a flooded house before you can repair it. Being at risk can make it very expensive or even impossible to insure. To discover the likelihood of flooding in your area, visit the Environment Agency's website.

When buying a house, whether it is next to a river or watercourse or not, the vendor is legally obliged, in the standard Law Society pre-contract enquiry form that every vendor must fill out for buyers' use, to declare whether there has been a flood during the time that he or she has owned it. It is illegal to misrepresent this information. If the sale goes ahead, you become what's known as a riparian landowner and have certain rights and responsibilities, including the obligation to accept flood flows through your land, even if caused by inadequate capacity downstream, as there is no common law duty to improve a watercourse.

What changes can I make?

It's very common to look at a house, love almost all of it, but wonder whether you could make a few changes. As many rural properties are listed or subject to strict planning regulations, it's worth discovering before you buy whether improvements or alterations would be permissible. We go into planning regulations in far greater detail in chapter four, but here's a rough outline of some of the most common instances where permission will be needed for work.

Listed buildings

If the property is listed, any alteration that affects its character is not permitted. The interior and exterior of all listed buildings are covered and structures in the grounds may also be included. Run your ideas past your conservation officer to see whether they might be possible.

Conservation areas

Whether or not it contains listed buildings, a local authority can designate part of a town a conservation area. With a few minor exceptions, it is illegal to demolish any building within such an area or alter its external appearance without prior consent from the planning department. This extends to the garden, too.

Planning permission

This is needed before carrying out any alteration that affects the use or siting of

Homes by the coast or inland that are listed are subject to strict planning regulations.

buildings or other structures. Any development that does not blend with its surroundings may also require consent. Usually, it is extensions or conversions that need consent, but even building a garden wall can be subject to approval if, say, it blocks a right of way.

In England and Wales, you will not usually require planning permission if you do not exceed the permitted development limit for your property (50–70 cubic metres, depending on where you live). But if the property has already been extended, you may not be able to do more work. Notable exceptions are homes in conservation areas and listed buildings. For these, check with your local authority conservation officer.

Conservatories built at ground level measuring under 30 square metres are also exempt from planning permission, provided that the safety glazing requirements of building regulations are adhered to. It is wise to speak to your local authority planning office before making any plans.

Second time around

It is vital to revisit the property before buying and to use your head, not your heart. If you fell in love with a property at the first viewing, it was probably its atmosphere and the lifestyle it suggested – alfresco meals on the terrace on summer evenings or a roaring log fire for winter days – that swayed you. The second viewing is a chance to divorce yourself from your emotional reaction, think practically and work out whether this house can really work for you and your family.

What to do

Conduct a thorough inspection. Use the lay person's survey below to inspect any areas you didn't look at on the first viewing.

- Run the showers to check water pressure and the hot taps to see if the boiler works. Find out how old the boiler is and when it was last serviced, and ask about the plumbing and when the house was last rewired. Take a note of where and how many plug sockets there are in each room. Do not be afraid to poke about in built-in cupboards to see how big they are, sniff for damp and find out where meters are hidden. Check that the windows open and close easily and that frames are not rotten. Take measurements to see whether your existing furniture would fit. If you can, peep under carpets to see what state floorboards are in or whether original floor tiles are hidden beneath. Find out whether fireplaces work and when the chimney was last swept. If possible, explore the loft or attic space. Notice the condition of roof trusses – are there signs of rot or infestation? – and whether the house is insulated.

- Outside, walk around the boundary and notice how close neighbours are. In summer, this could mean noise or lack of privacy. Check any outbuildings for their condition and current usage.

- Find out if planning permission has been granted (but not yet acted on) for any part of the house or its outbuildings. If you plan to work from home, existing permission to convert a cowshed into an office could be just what you are looking for.

- If you are buying a house that has been radically altered or extended recently, check that all the right planning permission was granted and building regulations adhered to. If you have been told that the property is guaranteed against events such as damp or beetle damage, your solicitor should gather all the relevant certificates and check their authenticity.

🐦 If you are feeling outgoing, call on neighbours to introduce yourself. Tell them you are very interested in buying the property and ask them about the neighbourhood, its facilities and what life is like there at different times of the year. They may be able to pass on useful information and give a valuable insight into the property and/or its surroundings. You will also get a quick idea of whether you will 'fit in' with the locals.

When to go

If you first visited during the week, try to go at a weekend, to see if traffic or noise levels are different. Similarly, if you went in broad daylight, try visiting in the evening, to see what lighting and access are like and whether parking is more difficult. Rooms will also feel different by night. A small room that was cosy by day may seem oppressively small at night, or a room that felt big and sunny at lunchtime may feel gloomy and cavernous by the evening. If it's winter, throw the windows open and listen, to get a feel for what noise levels may be like in summer.

Who else should view the property?

To get an idea of what you are taking on *before* you make an offer, you can instruct a surveyor to visit the house and give a valuation of repair. This typically costs a few hundred pounds. Alternatively, ask a specialist builder or architect to assess it, drawing their attention to any potential problems you spotted on the first viewing. They will probably quote for free, in the hope of winning the job. You could also approach your local conservation officer. They don't generally make this kind of visit, but it's worth asking, especially if the property presents major challenges or is of special interest.

On a second viewing, ask about the plumbing and run taps to check water pressure.

CHAPTER FOUR

Property surveys

You wouldn't buy a car without test driving it first, so don't even consider buying a property without getting a survey done before you commit yourself legally. A survey helps you make a reasoned and informed judgement on whether or not to proceed with the purchase, assess whether the property is priced reasonably and be clear what decisions and actions should be taken before contracts are exchanged. In some cases, the surveyor's report may even enable you to renegotiate the price.

Before you exchange contracts, do your homework by instructing a chartered surveyor to visit the property. He will consider whether the agreed price is reasonable, whether there are drawbacks that you may not be aware of and if so, what you need to do about them.

What type of survey do I need?

Mortgage valuation report

This is simply a report on the property's market value. It is often a minimum requirement to obtain a mortgage and evaluates whether the property is worth its asking price. You cannot rely on this report to answer your questions on the condition of the house. It is prepared for the lender and answers only the lender's questions concerning the appropriate security for your loan. It is therefore important to arrange a proper survey. The Consumers' Association *Which?* magazine and the Council of Mortgage Lenders recommend that you get a homebuyer survey and valuation (HSV) or a building survey. A mortgage valuation report typically costs £100–£250.

What a homebuyer survey and valuation includes

1   The property's general condition.
2   Any major fault, in accessible parts of the property, that may affect its value.
3   Urgent and significant matters that need assessing before exchange of contracts and recommendations for any further inspections.
4   Results of any damp tests on walls
5   Comments on damage to timbers, including woodworm or rot

6   Comments on the existence and condition of damp proofing, insulation and drainage
7   Recommended rebuilding costs for insurance purposes – in the event of a fire, for example.
8   The value of the property on the open market.

The homebuyer survey and valuation (HSV)

Often called the homebuyer service, this survey is intended for particular types of home: houses, flats and bungalows that are conventional in type and construction and apparently in reasonable condition. If you're buying a tumbledown farmhouse or a converted cattle shed, this is not the right survey for you.

The survey focuses on essentials: defects and problems that are urgent or significant and have an effect on the value of the property. It also covers the general condition of the property, looking at damp proofing, insulation, drainage and any damage to timbers caused by woodworm or rot.

Your attention will be drawn to any points that your legal advisers should be aware of and other relevant considerations concerning safety, the location and the environment.

The concise report covers the building inside and outside, the services and the site. Unlike a building survey, it also provides a valuation. If you need to take some action before going ahead with the purchase, this is signalled clearly, so you can't say you weren't warned! Expect to pay from £250 to £1,000, depending on the size of the property.

Other services a surveyor can offer when carrying out a standard homebuyer survey

If you have a particular concern – is the property suitable for a disabled person, say – the surveyor will keep this in mind during the inspection. Where necessary, he or she may offer additional services: providing a schedule of minor defects for later discussion with a contractor, or arranging for testing of mains services by suitably qualified specialists, for example.

Building survey

Formerly called a structural survey, a building survey is suitable for all residential properties and provides a full picture of their construction and condition. It is a more in-depth survey than the homebuyer survey.

What type of property needs a building survey? Anything that is of an unusual construction, regardless of its age; a house that is dilapidated, that has been extensively altered or where a major conversion or renovation is planned; plus all listed buildings and properties built before 1900.

What a building survey includes

1 Major and minor faults.
2 The implication of any faults and possible cost of repair.
3 Results of any testing of walls for damp.
4 Comments on the existence of damp proofing, insulation and drainage.
5 Extensive technical information on the construction of the property and details about the materials used.
6 Information on the location.
7 Recommendations for any further special inspections.

This type of survey doesn't follow a set format like a homebuyer survey, but is usually tailored to the client's requirements. The report includes extensive assessment of the condition of the property, technical information on construction and materials and details of the whole range of defects, major to minor, with advice for remedial works. It will look at specific problems and identify possible causes, advise on the likely consequences, make proposals on what can be done to solve or alleviate the situation and estimate the likely cost to rectify or investigate further. This type of survey costs £500–£1,500, depending on the size of the property.

Specialist surveys and engineers' reports

In some instances, a survey will highlight a problem that needs more thorough investigation by an engineer or specialist surveyor. Often, the surveyor can recommend a specialist to do this, or you can track one down yourself (call the Royal Institution of Chartered Surveyors helpline). Chartered engineers and specialist surveyors can offer advice on an array of specific problems. Here's a run-down of some of the issues that may affect a rural property and for which you might need advice.

Asbestos

What is it? Asbestos is a building material widely used over the past 100 years and particularly in the past 50 years, until it was banned in the late 1990s.

What type of house is it found in? Asbestos is a relatively modern material, so many people assume that a period property will be free of it, but many homes contain asbestos without the owners being aware of its presence. Most people know what an asbestos roof looks like, but asbestos can also be found in a range of relatively common building products, including roofing material, wall panels, some insulation materials used to lag hot water pipes and cylinders, and some Artex-type wall and ceiling coverings.

Why can it be problematic? It can cause lung cancer if inhaled as a dust; disturbing the material can produce dust.

Positive action Your building survey may highlight a potential problem with asbestos and recommend that an asbestos survey be carried out. The first stage involves a surveyor identifying any areas that might contain asbestos and writing a report proposing further action, together with an estimate of costs. You should budget on around £400 for the report. Next, a definitive survey is carried out, noting each area where asbestos may exist and samples taken for testing. This will cost more, depending on the number of samples taken.

The final step depends very much on the results of the survey, any legislative requirement to remove the asbestos and your wishes. In some cases a decision to remove the asbestos may be taken, in other cases it may be decided to leave the asbestos in situ and just ensure that the building is managed in a way that does not disturb it. Removal of asbestos from a building is very complex and costly. It should only be carried out by a licensed contractor who will ensure that it is done safely and that the asbestos, once removed, is taken to a licensed disposal site.

Cesspools and septic tanks

What are they? Cesspools are holding tanks for waste water and sewage and need to be emptied regularly, sometimes as often as every month. Septic tanks provide simple two-stage treatment of waste water and sewage before it filters out and soaks away into the ground.

What type of house has them? Usually rural properties that are a long way from a public sewer network.

Why can they be problematic? Typically, cesspools were not designed for and cannot cope with the amount of water generated by modern life – from washing machines, dishwashers and daily baths and showers. They can start to leak and, if this comes to the notice of the local authorities or Environment Agency, the cesspool will be subject to an order to be repaired or replaced. With older septic tanks the soakage system may well be inadequate for the same reasons or it could be choked and need clearing.

Positive action Other than a quick visual inspection from the outside to gauge the age and likely condition, there is very little that can be readily surveyed or tested without emptying the system and cleaning it out.

This is of course an expensive operation, normally done only if there are serious concerns. Again, your building survey may alert you to a problem here, but even if you have commissioned a detailed drainage report, it will not include this level of inspection unless specifically requested.

Damp

What is it? The most common type is rising damp. Moisture from the ground rises, by capillary action, up the walls. The moisture often carries salts that are deposited on the face of the wall when the moisture evaporates. Rising damp only extends up to one metre above ground level – capillary forces cannot lift the moisture any higher.

Penetrating damp is caused by moisture permeating the roof or walls.

What type of house has it? Any type. Normally walls are protected against rising damp by a damp-proof course built into the wall, but very old properties did not have damp-proof courses at all. Even where they do exist in older properties, the courses may have become ineffective. Any property where the outside ground level is raised above the damp-proof course (or above interior floor level) – called 'bridging' – is also more likely to be affected.

Penetrating damp can sometimes be caused by gutter or roof problems that allow rainwater to saturate walls. Any house with leaky gutters or clogged drainpipes is susceptible.

Why can it be problematic? Both rising and penetrating damp are usually quite evident – internal decorations become stained and damaged, plaster can become loose – but it can be difficult to pinpoint and cure the precise cause of the problem. Very often there is no quick or easy solution.

Positive action It is normal for a surveyor to employ a damp meter at random locations to check for any moisture in the internal walls. If the surveyor then requests a damp report, it is to confirm what type of damp it is, determine the extent of the problem and get an estimate for remedying it.

Poor drainage

What is it? Drainage from a building, as opposed to within a building, is invariably hidden underground. It includes the pipework that carries waste water and sewage away from the house, either to the mains drainage system or to the cesspool or septic tank.

What type of house has drainage problems? All houses can suffer from them, but the older and larger the property, the more likely.

Why can it be problematic? Out of sight usually means out of mind and so drainage tends to be ignored until it misbehaves. If a leaking drain is close to the house, the ground beneath the foundations can be weakened by water, resulting in subsidence. Leaking drains very often go undetected for decades, as they can only be checked via inspection chambers or manholes, and with older properties there may be few or none at all. In these cases, the only way to test and survey the drains is to dig holes and break into the pipes – this gets expensive. When drains are blocked or backing up from over-full cesspits or septic tanks, the system has to be unblocked, cleared or emptied at more expense.

Positive action If the surveyor notices cracking or other indications of foundation movement, which could be caused by leaking drains, he or she may order a drainage report. This may involve hydraulically testing several sections of drain for leaks or blockages. Or a small CCTV camera may be passed through the drains; the operator watches the picture as the camera progresses, to locate areas of damage or blockage. A CCTV survey can also be useful in determining the layout of a drainage system and identifying unknown or abandoned branches.

A drainage report would normally include a plan showing the layout of the drains, along with details of pipe diameters, depths below ground, results of water tests and findings of CCTV surveys.

Structural problems

What are they? Any fault or condition that adversely affects the fabric of the building – its roof, walls, timbers and beams.

What type of house has them? The older, the more likely. Years of general wear and tear and badly planned additions and 'improvements' over time can all play havoc with the structure of a period property.

Why can they be problematic? Structural problems can be complicated and expensive to put right, but cannot be ignored.

Positive action There are two types of report you can have done. A specific structural inspection is a visual inspection of a particular structural problem or concern. The report includes details of what was found, what further investigations may be necessary, any problems and what needs to be done to rectify them. It can also estimate costs for these.

A general structural inspection is similar to the above, except that the engineer or surveyor will inspect and report on the structural condition and adequacy of all the readily accessible load-bearing elements of the property, not just a particular problem area. It will therefore include roof structure, floors, walls, lintels and beams. It will also include the surrounding site in case there are any factors that indicate a risk to the foundations.

Inspections are usually carried out by a chartered engineer (CEng) who may be a member/fellow of the Royal Institution of Structural Engineers (MIStructE/FIStructE) or the Institution of Civil Engineers (MICE/FICE).

Timber damage

What is it? Fungal decay (dry rot and wet rot), plus damage caused by wood-boring insects.

What type of house gets it? Homes that are damp and poorly ventilated are particularly prone.

Why is it problematic? Fungal and insect attack can both cause serious damage to the structural timber and non-structural timber in buildings. Timber attacked by dry rot becomes dry and brittle – usually so weak that it can be broken up by hand.

Positive action The first steps in treating fungal decay are to discover and remove the sources of damp that are creating the ideal conditions for the outbreak, and to carry out exposure works to determine the extent of the damage. Repairs or replacement of badly affected timbers may be necessary. Following this it is usual to treat the timbers with an approved fungicide in order to prevent a future outbreak. Timbers badly weakened by wood-boring insects (woodworm) may also require repair or replacement plus insecticide treatment.

A typical timber report will include an inspection of all readily accessible timbers and recommendations for any necessary further exploratory works, repairs and treatment. Damp and timber reports are often carried out by the same specialist.

Subsidence and settlement

What are they? Subsidence usually refers to problems where a building is damaged by movement in the ground. Settlement refers to a failure of the components of a building.

What type of house is at risk? Homes built on clay soil, which can dry out and shift in hot weather, or close to large trees that suck up a lot of moisture from the soil are prone. The soil in the southeast is often clay – here one home in 50 has been affected by subsidence in the past 30 years.

Excessive rain can also disturb the ground and cause subsidence or ground slip.

Why is subsidence problematic?
It can make the entire property unsound and unsafe, making underpinning necessary. Underpinning involves pouring cement into the foundations of a property to prevent subsidence from recurring. It's an expensive, time-consuming exercise.

Positive action A subsidence or settlement report will establish the cause of the problem, whether it is likely to get worse and, if so, what actions should be considered to rectify it. Signs of subsidence and settlement in buildings are very common and can be the result of many causes. In some cases a building can reach a state of equilibrium and, if the problem is not too serious, nothing further will need to be done.

The timbers in old houses need regular checking and maintenance to prevent long-term problems.

Consent and planning

You've had an offer accepted on a property, got your survey done and know what problems you're facing. Still want to go ahead with the purchase? OK, assuming you were successful and hold the keys in your hand, it's now up to you to check carefully and, if necessary, apply for approval for any of the changes, extensions or even simple repairs you were planning to do to the building.

Regulations exist covering all kinds of work on all kinds of property. Before you start wielding your sledge hammer or extending your garden wall, find out if you need permission to do so first – you might be surprised by what is protected and what work simply isn't permitted. Below is a list of the most common restrictions and building controls that you will need to be aware of once in possession of a rural property.

Building regulations

Building regulations ensure the health and safety of people in and around buildings by setting out requirements for building design and construction. The regulations also promote energy efficiency. They apply to adding extensions, installing services, underpinning foundations, converting a loft space into living space and replacing windows (although building a conservatory or porch is exempt). The building regulations division of your local authority will be able to help you further.

Complying with building regulations is a separate matter from obtaining planning permission – and vice versa. Generally, if you are undertaking the work yourself, then the responsibility to ensure that it complies with building regulations is yours, but if you are using a team of builders, it is theirs – although check first with the building firm.

The Office of the Deputy Prime Minister publishes a useful booklet about building regulations, detailing exactly what works they cover. Read it at www.odpm.gov.uk.

Planning permission

As mentioned in chapter three, planning permission is needed before carrying out any alteration that affects the use or siting of buildings or other structures. Extensions or conversions will need consent – even building a garden wall can be subject to approval.

How do you apply? Contact the planning department of your local council and tell them what you plan to do. If they think you need permission, they will send you an application form. Ask if they foresee any difficulties with your plans at this early stage. If they do, you can amend your proposal, which might save time in the long run.

Draw up scale drawings of your existing and proposed dwelling, including elevations (the exact height measurements of everything from external walls to doors) and basic floor plans. These drawings need to be 100% accurate, so unless you are totally confident, get them done by a draughtsman or architect.

You don't have to make the application yourself. You can appoint an agent, for instance an architect, solicitor or builder, to do it. They will submit your plans with the appropriate fee. This varies, depending on the type of development proposed, but can be around £95.

The council should decide on your application within eight weeks. Large or complex applications may take longer.

Remember, too, that listed buildings have reduced permitted development rights: you might need planning permission for something that wouldn't normally need it if the building was unlisted – putting up a shed, for example. Check with your conservation officer.

Party wall regulations

The Party Wall etc Act 1996 applies throughout England and Wales and focuses on boundary walls and borders between properties. Specifically, it covers new building works at or astride the boundary between two properties, and structural work affecting an existing shared wall, including repairs. It also covers excavating or constructing foundations, depending on their depth and proximity to those of your neighbour.

A surveyor or your local authority planning office can advise you whether the work you are planning is governed by the act. If it is, you must serve statutory notice (one or two months, depending upon which part of the building is affected) on the adjoining owners and get agreement to the building programme before you start. The Office of the Deputy Prime Minister's website contains sample notice letters that you can use.

If your neighbours do not agree in writing, the best solution is to appoint an independent surveyor to draw up a party wall award. This will set out what can and cannot be done in accordance with the act. The owner who is carrying out the works normally pays the surveyor's fees, which vary according to the job. Find out more about the act at www.odpm.gov.uk.

Listed building controls

Owning a listed building means owning a little piece of history and, as such, carries greater responsibilities and is subject to greater restrictions than owning an unlisted house. You should consider yourself as a custodian of the building, not simply its owner: if you don't relish taking on the role of preserving it as it is, don't buy the house.

Controls for listed buildings do not set out to prevent change altogether, they just ensure it is managed with special care. This can limit what you might like to do to your home or how you might wish to change it. When work is allowed, your conservation officer may insist that you use compatible materials or appropriate conservation techniques.

Don't rely on estate agents' details to tell you whether your house is listed or not. Your solicitor should have told you when you were buying the house; if not, check with your local planning office.

What gets listed?

Buildings of special architectural and historic interest. Most are listed because of their architectural merit or age (all buildings built before 1700 surviving in anything like their original condition are listed, while only selected buildings from 1914 onwards are). There are currently 500,000 listed buildings in England and Wales.

What do the grades mean?

There are three grades of listing: II, II* and I. In Scotland, the grades are A, B, B (group) and C. Grade I is the highest grade in England and Wales. It typically applies to a major country house or something exceptional, like a building designed by a famous architect. Fewer than 3% of all listed buildings hold this grade.

Grade II* might be a particularly old building or one with important internal features, while grade II covers the vast majority (92%) of listed buildings, singled out for their age, architectural merit or even associations. Dylan Thomas's modest writing hut in Laugharne, Carmarthenshire, is grade II listed for its connection with the writer.

All grades need to apply for consent for any alteration work, but the higher grade I and II* buildings may be eligible for grants not available to grade II buildings.

What do I need consent for?

Any work to the inside and the outside, whatever the property's grade, if it affects its character. This means that even painting the building a different colour can require consent. Repair on a like-for-like basis should not need consent, in theory, whereas work like upgrading the windows, for example, would need listed building consent in order to comply with building regulations.

Listing also protects some fixtures and fittings – a chimney piece, for example, or a built-in dresser – as well as outbuildings, boundary walls and all other structures 'within the curtilage', that is, within the land belonging to the house. Construction that is within the curtilage, but entirely new and detached (a shed, for example), will not require listed building consent, but planning permission might be needed, where it wouldn't be needed for an unlisted building.

I'm planning work on my listed home; what should I do?

Contact the conservation officer in your local planning department as soon as possible to discuss your plans. The simplest way to apply for consent is to put matters into the hands of a suitably experienced professional (an architect, say) who can submit the appropriate application and negotiate with the local planning authority. You can, however, make an application yourself. It is not a good idea to do this for major works,

There are three grades of listing for buildings in England and Wales, designed to protect their special character. Before you start any work on a listed building you must contact your local conservation officer.

because the application process is complex, but you could do it for minor ones.

Before submitting an application it's a good idea to have an informal chat with your local conservation officer, who might be prepared to offer some general guidance. He or she will be able to give you an idea of what types of plans win consent and can point out any potential problems or difficulties with your application. Take this advice on board and, if need be, make amendments to your plans – it will save you time in the long run.

There is an application form to fill in, which you can get from your local authority – it generally comes with notes to help. You will also have to submit a site plan and reasonably detailed drawings showing the building as it is and as proposed, highlighting where changes are intended. You will need to add a supporting statement, as official guidelines say that applicants must be able to 'justify their proposals'. The local authority might then need more information, like a structural survey, to help assess the application.

Notification

In some circumstances, the council will have to inform certain official bodies of your plans. If your home is grade I or II* listed, then English Heritage (in England)

or the National Assembly of Wales (in Wales) will be notified.

If you are planning any work that involves demolition or an alteration that requires some demolition, then national amenity societies – the Society for the Protection of Ancient Buildings (SPAB), for example – must be notified, too, and they may ask to visit before commenting to the council.

Decisions and approval

If a planning application is uncontroversial and straightforward, a decision is usually reached within eight weeks. Approval lasts for a period of five years normally; once work has started, the approval is indefinite. Approval is usually subject to certain conditions. If you get permission to extend your property, for example, the consent may stipulate that the types of brick or mortar you plan to use are submitted for approval, too.

Homes in protected areas

Sometimes it's not just the type of home that you own that makes it subject to specific controls, but the area in which it is sited.

Conservation areas

Conservation area status was established by the Civic Amenities Act of 1967 to protect important localities. Each area usually contains a mix of listed and non-listed property.

In a conservation area, complete or substantial demolition of any structure larger than 115 cubic metres requires consent, as does removal of walls, fences or gates if they are over a certain height and depending on their location within your land.

The permitted development rights that normally apply to domestic buildings are restricted, too, so you'll need planning permission for things like adding dormer windows to a front roofscape or fitting a satellite dish that faces the road. Notice must also be given of the intention to lop or fell most trees. However, some building regulations are actually more flexible in conservation areas, acknowledging the need to balance good design and energy efficiency with building conservation. Call your local authority conservation officer before you start work.

National parks

Each of Britain's National Parks is managed by its own National Park Authority (NPA), which is responsible for development control. Contact the relevant NPA for advice on any works you are planning to a property within its boundaries.

World heritage sites

There are 25 'cultural' World Heritage Sites in Britain, including the entire city of Bath (the only complete city in Britain to be listed) and the centre of Edinburgh. This status brings extra planning constraints, but not a separate system of control. Your local planning office will be able to advise on what specific constraints apply to domestic property. Have a chat with them before you start any work.

Areas of outstanding natural beauty

Planning and development in an Area of Outstanding Natural Beauty (AONB) is the responsibility of the local authority within whose boundaries it falls. The primary objective of the AONB designation is to conserve and enhance the natural beauty of the area and this will be reflected in the local authority's plans.

Building regulations are often more flexible for homes in an AONB, acknowledging the need to balance good design and energy efficiency with building conservation. Contact the planning office of your local authority for advice.

Extending a 17th-century cottage

In 1994 Frances Iley bought a 17th-century listed property in the Oxfordshire town of Charlbury. It had been updated with ugly modern rendering and mass-produced brown-stained window frames, but was a bargain and had great potential. It adjoins what was once a pub (now a house), and despite being surrounded by other houses, Frances has significantly extended it. With only limited ground space, she managed to add a 'concealed' single-storey extension that transforms the three-bedroom cottage into an open-plan L-shaped house with a glass walkway and central courtyard garden.

Where did your inspiration come from? Partly out of necessity and partly because I loved the idea of having some sort of veranda. The basic house was small and not very special, but the big attraction was that it was cheap and had plenty of open land behind it. Then six months after I moved in permission was given to develop that land for two new houses. I was stuck with a bog-standard house with no view and couldn't afford to move. The only option was to turn it into something worth staying in. But it also had to provide privacy from the surrounding houses and meet the neighbours' approval.

What were your priorities in planning the new layout? I wanted a house that would feel comfortable when it was full of people. Houses also need to keep changing according to the time of year, the ages of your children, people coming to stay, elderly parents needing their own rooms

and perhaps wanting wheelchair access. So I was thinking about each area being able to change its use as time went on. Both halves of the house have one potentially self-contained end that could be let to a tenant, or provide somewhere for my mother to live one day.

It has been designed to provide easy access everywhere. There are glazed doors that lead from the sitting room into the new walkway, so it feels like one big space. The floor level is completely flush from the sitting room to the walkway and out onto the decking, and then across to the kitchen, so when all the doors are open, the boundaries vanish completely between the house and the garden.

What did you have to do to keep the neighbours happy? The neighbours behind wanted the roof line kept low. This meant digging down into the garden to avoid losing ceiling height. They didn't want to be overlooked either, so the windows in the end wall are all arrow slits – just enough to let light in.

How hard was it to get planning permission and listed building consent?
The plans took about two years to complete because they kept saying no to all the glass in the roof and doors as they thought it was too modern. For the design of the main house I used a local architect who specialises in conservation work and knew how to keep the planners happy – for instance, by using a barn-style timber framework rather than industrial-style metal. At one point the planners were distracted by a huge external gleaming chrome chimney I was contemplating for the sitting room and accepted other unusual aspects of the design as long as I dropped the chimney. They were also worried about the glass roof on the new hall – partly because they thought it might look like a conservatory and also because it had to meet heat conservation requirements.

Building regulations allow you to add a certain amount of glazed space to a building, to prevent lots of heat lost through glass into the environment. The proportion of glass against the size of the building is taken into consideration by using a calculation for the entire house, checking how much glazing there is and whether it is single or double glazed. Because our house has one blind wall with no windows in it, this meant it brought down the house's total amount of glazing and just about allowed us to have the glass roof. Removing one single glazed window and replacing it with a double glazed one also helped create the right ratio of glass to wall. We fitted a new boiler, which is more efficient than an old model, and this worked in our favour in terms of heat conservation.

How did being listed directly influence your plans? I had slightly more flexibility than most listed building owners because my house is only listed by association (being attached to an old pub), but the design of the joinery and colour of the paintwork still had to be agreed. I even had to get approval to renovate the greenhouse, because it is attached to the garden wall, and although the wall is new, it is attached to the house, which is listed.

Finding the right workforce

Even if you are an experienced renovator or seasoned DIY enthusiast, it is likely that any work you undertake on your property will involve enlisting specialist help. From a surveyor to a builder, read on to learn how to find the best person for the job.

See chapter nine for contact details of all the professional organisations mentioned here.

Surveyor

What do they do?

Primarily, they assess property that you are interested in buying – its value for money and general condition. They can also suggest remedial works, while specialist surveyors can compose detailed reports on specific issues like damp or subsidence. If you are undertaking structural changes to your property, you will need to use a structural surveyor, who will work closely with the architect, project manager and builder. Surveyors can also draw up basic plans for submission to the local council when planning permission is needed, and some will also project manage a build if required.

How do I find one?

If you only want a homebuyer survey done and are taking out a mortgage, your mortgage lender will often arrange the survey for you using one of its affiliated surveyors. If you are organising the survey independently, whether it's a homebuyer survey or building

survey, the Royal Institution of Chartered Surveyors (RICS) can help you find a chartered surveyor in your area. It has an online member directory with currently 19,290 firms offering surveying services, or you can call its contact centre. You will be given the names of RICS qualified members in your area.

If you have a particularly old or unusual property, you can narrow down your search to surveyors qualified and experienced to do the work you need. The RICS lists surveyors covering more than 160 specialisms, including conservation specialists, who will be able to advise on listed buildings, and experts in boundary or party wall act issues.

Make sure you use only a qualified RICS member, who can offer independent, impartial advice and who follows strict codes of practice. A chartered surveyor will use the letters MRICS or FRICS – meaning they are either a member or a fellow of RICS. A technical surveyor will use the letters TechRICS – meaning they are a qualified technical member of RICS. Slightly fewer academic criteria are needed to become a TechRICS.

Architect

What do they do?

A lot. From simply drawing up plans to submit for planning permission, to involvement at every stage of the project, including co-ordinating a team of consultants such as landscape architects, engineers, quantity surveyors, interior designers, builders and subcontractors. You can select all or part of an architect's service, from an initial design discussion through to the final delivery of the project on site.

Architects are trained problem solvers and skilled visualisers. If you are planning a job that is too big or complex for just you and your builder, then it is time to employ one. They will advise on whether what you are attempting is achievable, consider what is best for the property and how to do this within your budget. They will also have an idea of what kinds of changes will get planning approval and which are more likely to be turned down.

Architects' fees can be based on a percentage of the total construction cost, on time expended or a lump sum. For simply drawing up plans they might charge around £55 an hour, but working on a project from concept to completion will cost 10% or more of the total cost of the renovation work. Get estimates from a couple of different architects: charges can vary drastically depending on their current workload. Architects and designers are market led and in a boom time they can be booked up for months in advance, which gives them the upper hand when negotiating fees. It makes sense to shop around.

You might want to see if you can negotiate a fixed price. For projects of less than £20,000 most architects prefer to charge by the hour, but a set fee could save you several hundred pounds. Check whether the fee includes all the necessary plans, too. The architect may charge extra for reworking plans, so make sure any redesigns are included in the fixed fee.

How do I find one?

If you own an old property, you will need to find an architect who knows about old buildings and their components; someone who has come across green oak joinery, wattle and daub walls or thatched roofs before. A young, recently qualified architect might not be so well versed in these traditional construction techniques.

Choose someone who thinks in imperial not metric – that's what your property's measurements would have been in – and who can draw properly, rather than using computer-assisted drawing (CAD). Get quotes from a couple of firms, ask for references and go to see other projects the architect has worked on before you make your decision. Above all, talk to your intended architect. It is important that you get on.

If you are looking for a sensitive conservation architect to oversee the repair of a complex historic house, talk to the SPAB. They can make referrals and advise, but not recommend. Or contact the relevant architectural society. The Georgian Group or the Victorian Society, for example, might be able to help.

The Royal Institute of British Architects (RIBA) can recommend by area and expertise and has a good website. Its Architects Accredited in Building Conservation (AABC) branch also details members who are knowledgeable and experienced in the conservation of historic buildings.

Builder or tradesman?

How do I find one?

Finding the right builder is at the heart of any successful project on a rural property. The wrong builder can cripple your bank balance and send your blood pressure soaring. The right one will make the project sail along seamlessly. Good builders love buildings and know all about them – essential when working on a period property. If you take as much care selecting a builder as you would a nanny, you are less likely to go wrong.

Ask around. Your local conservation officer might be able to recommend someone, or a friend or neighbour may have recently had work done to a high standard. You could try the Federation of Master Builders, or Heritage Information, an online fund of restoration information including experts, consultants and skilled tradespeople who are all vetted. The Association for Environment Conscious Building can recommend local builders and experienced craftspeople, from thatchers to joiners. The Heritage Building Contractors Group has a list of reputable companies.

Check references and look at other jobs the company has done. When you have three builders shortlisted, detail the works you want done and ask them to quote. Don't simply opt for the cheapest – expect to pay proper fees. If you find a builder with expert knowledge of your kind of property, but he is booked up, wait for him. Don't just employ another firm. Expertise is more important than availability.

Project manager

What do they do?

They manage a building project, running the site from start to finish, ensuring it complies with building regulations and permissions, hiring contractors and tradesmen, scheduling works and making sure they meet a pre-agreed budget and time scale. They also pay wages, order materials and are often on site six days a week, from 7am until dusk, and will take the rap if things go wrong. They usually charge about 10% of the cost of the project.

How do I find one?

Your local planning office or builder might be able to recommend one. Look in the phone book as many project managers now advertise. Remember to check references.

Architectural historian

What do they do?

As the term suggests, this is someone with specialist knowledge of architecture and its history. They will often have studied a related field at university and may specialise in the vernacular traditions of an area or in specific types of building – lighthouses or cottages, for example.

If you have an old property of special interest, an architectural historian might be interested in examining it. They can read your house at a glance and will be able to explain its history, when and how additions or alterations were made, what rooms and features were used for and they may even uncover hidden features like door frames or windows.

How do I find one?

Any architectural society or local history group in your area may be able to help, or visit the library for publications on local architecture and trace the author from there. Your local authority conservation officer might also be able to advise. Alternatively, contact the House Historians, a professional architectural history practice specialising in interpretative reports on historic buildings. Reports contain an account of the building's entire historical development, together with further evidence in the form of maps, drawings and photographs and cost from £250.

CHAPTER FIVE

5

Grants, funding and budgeting

Calculating how to fund a move to the countryside is an essential process in making that leap successfully. Only the most fortunate individuals sell their city residence for a fat profit and can buy a country house outright. For most, moving to the countryside is not that simple financially. Some pockets of the country still offer inexpensive property, but many do not, and it is a mistake to assume that moving to the countryside equals buying a cheap house.

You may need to borrow more money on your existing mortgage or choose to take out a new one. If you are buying a dilapidated home or converting a property not built for domestic use, you will find that fewer lenders are ready to step forward with a loan. In some instances, you may be eligible for a grant from English Heritage or another body for proposed work, but grants are generally not that easy to come by. Whatever your financial state, you will need to budget carefully, considering everything from increased mortgage repayments to removal costs, renovation work to stamp duty.

Raising finance for your home

Mortgages

Taking out a mortgage on your new rural home will be subject to its condition.

If the property is habitable – that is, with a sound roof, a working kitchen and indoor bathroom – most lenders will be happy to offer you a loan. You then have the choice of a repayment or endowment mortgage and hundreds of potential packages to choose from. Reading about mortgages isn't exactly scintillating, but thorough research on the internet and newspaper money pages will ensure that you get the best deal and save money in the long run.

It's a good plan to have some idea of how much you can borrow before you start house hunting so that you know which properties are within – and outside – your price range. It's also sensible to have secured your mortgage before you put in an offer. It saves time and won't hold up the sale, which makes you and your offer more attractive to the vendor.

Three things to consider when taking out a mortgage on a rural home

1   Does the property need work? Borrowing an additional amount on top of the agreed sale price could be the cheapest way to access a lump sum for improvements.

2   Will your earning capacity be reduced by moving to the countryside? Make sure you can meet the repayments based on your future earnings, not your current salary.

3   Rural properties generally require more maintenance than urban. If you are mortgaged up to your eyebrows, will you have any money left to spend on upkeep?

Mortgages for wrecks

If you want to take on a building that is uninhabitable, it's harder to get a mortgage. A handful of lenders offer specialist packages, tailored to the needs of the renovator. Try the Norwich and Peterborough Building Society, which lends to restoration projects. Or the Ecology Building Society – it specialises in loans to people undertaking renovation on derelict properties. It lends nationally, covering the whole of Britain and you do not have to be 'green' to get an Ecology mortgage. While many of their borrowers have environmental concerns, others simply want to rescue a derelict property to make into a home.

Buildstore, which specialises in self-building projects, has arrangements with several lenders who will also loan for restoration, although it helps if you're using one of Buildstore's approved project managers. The advantage to you is that it makes accessing your loan easier. Typically, a lender will agree a total loan, with a large chunk upfront to buy the property, then further amounts released as key stages of the work are completed. Before each new amount is released, a valuer usually has to visit the property to confirm that the work has been done and that the market value has appreciated, which costs around £50 a time. With a mortgage and project manager through Buildstore, these visits are unnecessary – money is released on request.

See chapter nine for contact details of the organisations mentioned.

Grants

You will not always have to shoulder the financial burden of repairing or restoring your home alone. Depending on the age, style and importance of your home, you may be eligible for a grant.

Where to go for help

Don't assume that because you own a listed building you are more likely to get help. Grants for listed buildings are increasingly hard to find. On the whole, they are more readily given to buildings in charitable ownership than private. Similarly, the highest grade buildings – grade I and II* – in need of repair will tend to get the grants in preference to a grade II property in private ownership and reasonable condition.

English Heritage offers grants to grade I and II* buildings on a case-by-case basis. The proposed work must cost £10,000 or more and successful applicants typically receive 40%–60% of repair costs and fees. English Heritage doesn't, however, tend to offer grants if the building has just changed hands, as the cost of work is assumed to have been reflected in the purchase price. English Heritage's funding priorities do not really benefit someone who has just bought a dilapidated listed building, since they favour buildings at risk, those without beneficial use – follies or redundant barns, for example – or those that have been in the same family for more than 30 years.

The Heritage Economic Regeneration Scheme (HERS) has grants to restore home and business premises in conservation areas. This scheme is run by English Heritage. Contact your local planning office to see if your home qualifies.

Local authorities may have their own historic buildings grant funds, but they are generally quite modest (£1,000–£2,000 per application). This is sometimes repayable if you sell the property within a fixed period from completion of works (often three to five years). Ask at your local planning office.

The Department for Environment, Food and Rural Affairs (Defra) offers grants to individuals restoring or converting agricultural buildings, to help preserve our agricultural heritage. Everything from dovecotes to cowsheds have been restored with Defra money. A straightforward restoration is likely to qualify for a higher percentage grant than a conversion, but even if you are intending to convert a building you may be entitled to help. Grants usually run into tens of thousands.

Historic Scotland awards more than 100 grants to private owners and others each year, to help towards the cost of repairing many of the nation's outstanding historic buildings. In return, owners must insure and maintain the building and allow some access to visitors.

The Georgian Group gives small donations towards the repair and restoration of Georgian buildings through the Cleary Fund.

The Society for the Protection of Ancient Buildings (SPAB) is primarily an advisory body, but it may be able to make small contributions towards temporary emergency work in deserving cases.

SPAB also has a small fund for the repair of almshouses and a Thomas Hardy fund that can contribute to the cost of repair to buildings with a Hardy connection.

Local conservation societies may be prepared to contribute.

The Architectural Heritage Fund publishes *Funds for Historic Buildings in England and Wales – A Directory of Sources* that includes a number of statutory, public and other sources. Most only help charitable or public bodies, but some information will apply to individual owners of historic buildings.

Other costs

There is more to buying a home than just covering the purchase price. You will need to factor in money for everything from legal fees to the removal firm's charges, so budget carefully and remember these extra expenses.

Estate agents' fees

If you sell your city home through an estate agent, they will take anything from 1.5–3% of the final purchase price, depending on where you live (fees rise the further south you go, with London the highest). Many people selling through an estate agent assume that these fees are fixed and do not think to question them. In fact, they are open to negotiation, so don't be afraid to haggle with your estate agent. Be prepared to use another firm if they will not come to an agreement that suits you. There are always plenty of estate agents out there eager to have your business.

Stamp duty

This is a government tax on properties that sell for over £60,000. Properties that sell for £60,000–£250,000 are liable to 1% stamp duty, for £250,000–£500,000 it's 3% and for those over £500,000 it's 4%.

Legal fees

You will need a solicitor to carry out searches on the property as well as handle the purchase of your new home and the sale of your existing one. Most charge a flat rate for conveyancing work, starting at around £500.

Borrowing set-up costs and interest

If you are taking out a mortgage, there will be lenders' fees. Some charge a fee to secure your mortgage package (often around £200) and they may also want to carry out a mortgage valuation report, which costs around £100–£250.

Land Registry costs

It costs approximately £80–£100 to register your ownership of your new property with the Land Registry, which is done on completion.

Removal costs

Unless you have a van and a great deal of time and energy, transporting your worldly possessions to your new home is a job for a removal firm. Firms offer a range of services, from simple loading and transportation to a wrapping, packing and unpacking service. The average cost of removals for a three-bedroom semi-detached house in England and Wales is around £400, but this will vary widely depending on the size of your home, distance to move and value of your possessions. Check that the removal firm has adequate insurance. Most removal firms offer limited liability cover, because they do not know the value of the goods they are transporting, so it is also sensible to take out your own insurance cover greater than the limits set out in the removal company's terms and conditions.

Storage

If you are initially moving to a furnished rented home, or simply to a much smaller house, you may need to put some of your furniture into storage. There are plenty of storage facilities around, offering high-quality and secure units. Costs vary depending on the size of the unit, the access you need to it, the length of time you wish to hire it for and insurance. You can hire a 40ft container for a month for around £50, excluding insurance.

Rent

One way of relocating is to rent a property first, before buying a home. The rent may be less than your current mortgage repayments, but it may not – don't forget to take it into account. You will probably also be asked to pay a security deposit, usually around a month's rent, and pay the monthly rent in advance, not arrears, so just securing the property involves spending a hefty amount up front.

Redecoration

Making your new property feel like home involves spending money. It's inevitable. You may need to buy more furniture or redecorate extensively. It might be possible to buy some of the previous owner's fixtures and fittings, which can be economical – talk to your estate agent or the vendor about this. When budgeting for even the most basic repairs, improvements or redecoration work, calculate how much you think it will cost, then double it. If you manage to do the work for less than you budgeted, great. In practice, though, most jobs end up costing more than you might at first imagine, so allowing more money is sensible and protects you from nasty financial surprises later down the line.

Repairs to beautiful original features such as a leaded light window are worthwhile to keep them in working order.

Budgeting for a project

Restoring a wreck

With old buildings in a poor state of repair, it is often difficult to predict how much work – and therefore how much money – will be needed to restore them. Each new stage of work can reveal problems that you may not have budgeted for, but that require attention. A good builder, surveyor or architect will have a reasonable idea of what to expect, where problems may arise and how much it will cost to fix them, but they need to see the property in its intact state. For example, once you start pulling off plaster from walls with problems, it's difficult to trace their cause. Find out as much as you can about the property's condition before you start work. Get a full building survey and any further follow-up surveys or reports done. Spend money at this stage and you are less likely to be surprised by additional expenses later.

You will need to use experienced builders or specialists, who will charge more. You may be required to use specific materials made using traditional techniques – again, more expensive. Natural roofing slate, for example, can cost 50% more than imitation slate. Get detailed quotes from all tradesmen and builders and factor in an additional 15% as a contingency. Always remember the difference between a quote and an estimate, too. An estimate is usually verbal and non-binding, offering a rough idea of costs, while a quote should be in written form, with work fully itemised, and it is legally binding.

If you are using an architect or surveyor to help plan the renovation, there may be additional costs if the planning office rejects your initial proposals and you need a revised set of plans. Each one can cost from £200 to £600, depending on complexity, so it's a good idea to try to negotiate unlimited redesigns from your architect as part of a fixed fee.

If the property is listed, certain types of work for which you have listed building consent are VAT exempt; repairs are still subject to 17.5% VAT, although approved alterations are potentially zero-ratable. The criteria for exemption is complicated and can vary regionally, but you should always get listed building consent first for any work where zero-rating is sought. According to recent research by *The Sunday Times*, owners of listed buildings are paying more than £250 million per year in unnecessary VAT. The Listed Property Owners' Club publishes a useful leaflet on this subject.

Conversions

The appeal of converting an old building such as a chapel or barn is that you are buying an interesting, historical building, but the complications of converting it for domestic use mean that it will inevitably end up costing more than building a new home from scratch. An old building in need of conversion is often reasonably inexpensive to buy but, because it was never designed for human habitation, turning it into a functional home will almost certainly push up expenditure. It's not uncommon to end up spending half as much again as you originally estimated.

Converting a property is a time-consuming project – a year at the very least – and for much of that time it will remain uninhabitable, so you will need to budget for your existing mortgage or the cost of renting.

When preparing for this kind of project, factor in the cost of hiring an architect to draw up plans, builders who are experienced in this kind of work (and therefore may charge more than less specialist builders) and, unless you plan to be on site every day and have experience of running a large project, a project manager, too. He or she will command at least 10% of the overall project costs. This may seem like a lot, but is money well spent. Project managing is a complex job and, if you are inexperienced and attempt it yourself, it could end up costing you even more in budget and schedule overruns.

Even if you do get planning permission for your project, it may come with a long list of restrictions, like using only traditional materials, which can cost three times as much as their off-the-shelf modern equivalents.

Allow a contingency. Treat it as an essential part of your costings, not an optional luxury. Set aside 10–15% of your overall budget so that you are covered for unexpected problems, hiring more labour or urgent works.

The hidden costs of restoration

If you are buying a property that is structurally sound but needs modernisation and refurbishment, you still need to budget carefully. You may not be employing troops of builders or an architect, but even installing a new kitchen or windows will need thought, possibly consent and often more money than you first planned to spend.

Building regulations now require that any building work makes your home more energy efficient, with the exception of homes that are listed or in conservation areas. This means, for example, that new windows must be double glazed, which will push up costs. The building control department of your local council can advise.

Your survey will have alerted you to any repairs that need urgent attention and may have included estimates of their cost. Rewiring and replumbing are substantial jobs typically done when updating an unmodernised house.

You should also consider how you furnish your property. A budget kitchen will look out of place in a grand Georgian country house, but you will have to pay much more for a bespoke wooden one that will suit it better.

Checklist

- Use appropriate materials for the age of your property.

- Factor in the larger scale of repairs. Any job will cost more in a sprawling country home than it does in a neat city terrace.

- Ensure all work is in keeping with the property's age and history, whether it is listed or not. These will make even the most simple repairs and improvements more costly than you might expect.

Renovating property for profit in the countryside

The trend for buying run-down houses, renovating them quickly and then selling them for a large profit is well established in Britain's cities. Many people have made a great deal of money developing property in this way. In the countryside, however, where every property is different and any house of character is likely to be listed, it is an altogether more risky enterprise.

Property development relies on a quick turnaround, something that is harder to achieve when working on a listed property or one in a conservation area, because you will need consent for each aspect of the work. To create a sensitive restoration, you should also spend time getting to know the property, researching its history, sourcing skilled builders and tradesmen and possibly waiting for them to be available. This kind of time investment is the enemy of a fast profit.

Property development also centres on using the least expensive materials to make the best possible finish, but listed building consent will insist that you repair on a like-for-like basis, using traditional, more expensive materials. With costs escalating, your resale profit will dwindle.

The rural market is far more seasonal than the urban, with a slow down in activity over winter and autumn. This means the timing of a development is crucial. If you complete it in autumn, when the market is beginning to slow, it could be another six months before you sell – an expensive delay.

While listed buildings are particularly problematic, do not make the mistake of thinking that converting a building would be lucrative, either. Although conversions command high prices, they pose just as many problems to the would-be developer. 'If you spot a barn that needs converting in the countryside and you think you can get planning permission, it's a two-year process from beginning to end,' says James Laing, head of the rural division of Strutt & Parker estate agents. 'Most people would have to invest all the money before they could sell their house as they would need somewhere to live while the work is taking place. It's also not easy to get mortgages to convert buildings and, if you are new to the area, you won't be familiar with the planning system, which can make winning permission harder.'

Next page: Renovating an old property like this takes time, money and patience.

CHAPTER SIX

Restoring your property

For many would-be country dwellers, moving to a nicely finished home is too easy. Their dream centres on renovating a wreck, nursing it back to life and basking in the satisfaction of having saved a historic building from ruin while creating a characterful home.

Restoring a wreck is the chance to get to know a historic building, take responsibility for every tiny job that will ultimately piece it back together and create a truly unique space. However, turning a wreck into a dream home is no easy task. It requires plenty of inspiration and research. It also demands a lot of hard work and devotion. Regardless of your level of experience in working on property, you will almost certainly need specialist advice and expertise at some point. Some of this can be bought; some you will want to discover for yourself by reading up or attending one of the many building conservation courses held around the country. That, after all, is part of the fun and where the ultimate satisfaction lies.

However big or small the project, there will be times when you think you were mad to have taken it on and others when you are flushed with pride at what you have achieved. All restorers say that working on a major restoration project is something of a roller-coaster ride – physically, emotionally and often financially. There are no guarantees with old houses. They reveal unexpected delights but also throw up unwelcome surprises, though if you have the time, money and patience, restoring an old house could be one of the most rewarding projects you will ever take on.

Researching the history of your property

Why research?

Understanding your property's history, construction and architecture is essential when undertaking restoration work. The more time you spend simply looking at the building, the more likely you are to understand how it developed, and the more you know about your home, the more likely you are to value it, appreciate its oddities and make sensible decisions for its restoration. You will also have the confidence to defend your proposed work at planning stage, which is helpful when it comes to getting consent. Remember, though, that some parts of your home may forever remain a mystery, and even the experts may not be able to explain why some odd piece of stone sticks out or why something is the way it is.

How to research

You can research the history of your house yourself or employ a professional architectural historian.

If you are doing it yourself, a useful starting point is the internet, which has lots of sites with information on historical houses. Visit the Building Conservation website, which has good articles and suggested further reading, or Heritage Information's site, an online resource for anyone restoring a historical building. It also has a bookshop and plans to set up an interactive searchable encyclopaedia of English architecture.

Visit your local library, too. It may have a photographic archive, which might include your property. There may be publications on local architecture as well as more general works. It is useful to read about the period in which your home was built, to understand how people lived and what they used their rooms for, as well as researching your area and its vernacular traditions. If your house is Victorian, look out for *The Victorian Society Book of the Victorian House* by Kitt Wedd (Autumn Press). The Society for the Protection of Ancient Buildings (SPAB) sells several books on dating houses, including *Discovering Your Old House* by David Iredale and John Barrett (Shire Publications, £6.99 plus £1.50 p&p).

Approach local conservation societies, which may have invaluable knowledge. Many operate at county level; for example, the Sussex Archaeological Society or the Somerset Vernacular Building Research Group. There are also numerous national societies that can advise or refer you to helpful booklets or publications. Try the Victorian Society, the Georgian Group, the SPAB or the United Kingdom Institute for Conservation. The Listed Property Owners' Club publishes useful background notes on historical housing.

If your building is listed, a good starting point can be English Heritage's 'list description', which gives the best official estimate of the date of your house and why it is listed. However, many entries are very brief.

It's wise to be cautious about what the estate agent, previous owners or local people tell you about the history. Also remember that date stones can be misleading – they may refer to only one phase of building, or in some instances may be the result of romantic Victorian imagination.

Talk to your conservation officer about old records or plans that might exist in local authority files. You could also contact the county records office and the census records.

If you would prefer to use an architectural historian, ask your conservation officer if he can recommend one, or contact the House Historians, a professional architectural history practice specialising in interpretative reports on historic buildings. See chapter nine for details.

When it comes to research at grass roots level, gently does it. Do not start chipping off plaster or carrying out other destructive investigations in your enthusiasm for finding out more about the building. Far too much permanent damage can been done by this misguided urge.

Restoring a grade II listed cottage in Sussex

Melanie and Roger Williams bought a dilapidated 16th-century grade II listed cottage in East Sussex that was home to the village post office until 1999. Hours of wallpaper and paint stripping have revealed the original lath and plaster walls and beautiful beams in the ceiling, while building work has opened up the attic and made the house warm and liveable.

How did you research the house's history?
Melanie: It was very straightforward. An architectural society had researched the estate the house is on some years ago and had done an in-depth study of our house, which the county records office copied for us. Then a local architectural historian visited. He dated the house to 1550. The only work that has been done on the house since then has been the single-storey building at the back, added during the 1700s. He also showed us details, like the original window in the kitchen that we hadn't realised was there. It was really interesting.

How did you find a good builder?
Roger: The conservation officer recommended him because he had experience of old houses. He knew how to use lime plaster, which we have here on our lath and plaster walls. He also knew all about the SPAB, whereas many we talked to had never heard of it, therefore he understood exactly what we were trying to achieve. We got several quotes and he was the most expensive, but that wasn't what we were concerned with. We wanted to restore the property well.

Did you get any advice during the project?
Melanie: We went on one of the SPAB's weekend courses, an introduction to the repair of old houses. That set us on the right path. Now we can talk with a bit of knowledge and we know what questions to ask. It gave us the confidence to find the right people.

The owners of this 16th-century cottage undertook thorough research into its history before beginning to restore it.

Keeping the character

Restoring an old property is not about giving an elderly structure a modern facelift using the latest super-efficient materials. Neither is it about creating a museum piece, where every inch of its fabric has been stripped back to the period when it was first built. Houses evolve throughout their lifetime, with each generation of occupants leaving its mark, and each addition potentially of value and interest.

Before you start work, here are some dos and don'ts.

DON'Ts

- **Don't** replace what you can repair. An honest, visible repair is better than a fake reproduction. Your aim is to retain as much of the original fabric of the house as possible. Replace only on a like-for-like basis, matching original materials and workmanship as accurately as you can. Always try to recycle materials and fittings elsewhere in the house, too.

- **Don't** think that you have to strip back every room to expose original details. Consider keeping later additions if they add to its history. It is important to remember that improvements would have been made to the property throughout its life. A 16th-century farmhouse will probably have original details like Tudor fireplaces, but it might also boast a Georgian facade or extension, a Victorian tiled floor or hearth and, less appealingly, 1950s light fittings and panelling that conceals the

beams. While the modern panelling could go, the other additions all add to the property's interest and deserve a place.

- **Don't** assume that all modern additions are bad. For example, you might be tempted to fit reproduction Edwardian light switches to your cottage rather than a modern equivalent, but smart brass fittings of that style would only have been seen in the richest homes, not a humble cottage. Most cottages didn't get electricity until as late as the 1950s, so it's obvious how inappropriate such fittings would be and it is much better to use a simple modern version.

- **Don't** attempt to make a simple house grand or a low-ceilinged cottage light and open plan. You should be buying a period home because you like its scalp-skimming beams, its rough and undulating walls, its uneven floor or small rooms. Work with what you have. Buy according to your needs, rather than trying to mould a house to them. If you like large rooms and tall windows, don't even think about snapping up a farm worker's cottage.

- **Don't** start ripping out carelessly. What may appear to be immediately disposable might offer clues to the house's original fabric. The contents of the roof or even the debris in a tumbledown room might tell you how the house was built and what materials used. Respect small details like latches, glass, guttering, windows and doors, which often reflect local building traditions and may be hard to replace.

Small details such as latches and door furniture may date back hundreds of years and should be preserved.

Part of the pleasure of owning an older property is being able to enjoy original features like this fireplace.

DOs

Do accept the inevitable signs of age that come with a period property. Regular maintenance and redecoration are essential, but aggressive cleaning, repointing and painting external joinery with brilliant white gloss will rob the property of its historic interest. The muted patina of history and benign neglect are preferable to the look of an over-restored house.

Do distinguish between reversible and irreversible alterations and take the reversible approach whenever possible. Painting the front door a different colour is reversible. Replacing it with a modern door is, too, but with some effort. Covering the house exterior with pebbledash render is irreversible. It can't be removed without irreparable damage to timber or brickwork.

Do respect the plan and original room divisions. Think of clever alternatives that avoid large-scale restructuring. For example, an alternative to knocking through two living rooms is to install double doors.

Do the minimum necessary to make the property liveable. Installing fancy security gates to a modest cottage is a modernisation too far.

Do research the vernacular traditions of your area. Find out about local building materials and styles and join local preservation trusts or the SPAB. The better informed you are about your home and its history, the better able you will be to make the right choices for its repair.

Do spend money on essentials first. Repairs to the fabric of the building can be expensive and depressingly mundane, but you cannot afford to ignore them. Decorating, on the other hand, can wait without any harm being caused to the building.

Do go slowly. Get to know the property before you call in the builders. If possible, live in it for a while to get a feel for its rooms, layout and atmosphere, and how it works for your family. Explore cellars, lofts, outbuildings – anywhere that might throw up clues about how the building was constructed and any problems it has. The more you know about your home, the better client you will be for professionals and builders, and the easier it will be for you to work with them.

A grade I listed house brought back to life

Northgate House in Bury St Edmunds was derelict when Joy and Gerard Fiennes took it on seven years ago. Two years of painstaking work, with the couple camping out in various rooms as it progressed, have restored it inside and out. Joy explains the detailed research and work that went into preserving its unique character.

What state was the house in when you bought it? It was derelict. There was water coming in through many different places. I spent the first year walking about the roof, unblocking drainpipes and gutters.

What's the history of your home? It's medieval with a Georgian exterior. In 1713, two medieval properties were simply built over. They were joined in the centre with a big hall and then a red brick skin encased the whole structure. They even roofed over the existing roof. If you go into the attic space, the original medieval beams are still there and you can see what shape the old roof was. We got an architectural historian to draw how it would have looked, explaining each layer. It helped make sense of the layout.

What was involved in keeping its character? The house is grade I listed, so we weren't allowed any pipework at the front. This meant we had to run pipes between floors and out to the rear of the building. We got traditional square downpipes made specifically. We also recycled old switches and repaired cracks in the panelling. We didn't replace anything, just recycled and repaired.

Was there anything you weren't allowed to do? We exposed a beautiful medieval ceiling in one room, but had to cover it up again, so it looked as it would have done in Georgian times. This was at the stipulation of English Heritage.

How did you choose colours for the interior? An architectural historian scraped some paint off the panelling and worked out that it had only been painted three times since 1713. The original colours were underneath – including a beautiful soft blue in the hall – which we simply matched to Farrow & Ball shades. We didn't use authentic colours everywhere. The Georgians liked some very bright shades. There was one turquoise we uncovered that I knew I could never live with!

Northgate House is now a B&B: to book call 01284 760469; www.northgatehouse.com.

Have you got what it takes to restore an old property?

You need more than just money and a set of plans to survive a restoration project, let alone enjoy it. Check this list to see if you have the right personality to deal with the challenge.

Patience

For the restorer, patience is a virtue. The most successful restorations are those undertaken slowly, with time spent getting to know the house, researching its past and planning the work. Do not expect instant results. Even getting planning permission or listed building consent for work can take a year.

Experience and/or enthusiasm

Experience and knowledge are, of course, invaluable, but it's surprising what can be achieved by a motivated amateur.
A willingness to learn and have a go are sometimes just as useful.

Vision

Vision is essential. When you are up to your ears in plaster dust, it is easy to lose sight of what you are trying to achieve. Keep an

If you take on the restoration of an old property like this you must be prepared to be patient and keep up your levels of enthusiasm and energy.

image of your future home in your mind's eye at all times and you will not lose heart.

Confidence

Confidence in your vision is also essential. You should never be put off because a job isn't easy or because your builder says it cannot be done. A considered confidence in your work will also prevent you from changing your mind halfway through.

Time-keeping skills

An ability to stick to deadlines and understand schedules is another useful trait. Determination to get the job done will keep you on site for that extra hour each day when others might head home and risk the project falling behind schedule as a result.

Energy

The amount of basic labouring work on any sizeable project is massive and easily underestimated. Just dealing with that can sap your energy – and that's before you tackle the more complex restoration work.

101

How to organise a major restoration project

There are a number of ways you can proceed, depending on the house's condition, your budget and the degree of involvement you wish to have.

If the house is basically habitable, but with a string of repairs and improvements needed, make a list of the defects you have found and try to list them in order of priority. Then group them together in order of trades, so that you can decide whether a general builder is appropriate or whether you need only a couple of specialists – for jobs like repairing stained glass or rethatching the roof. Have a look in the resources section in chapter nine for useful websites or organisations that hold registers of contractors, consultants and craftspeople.

If you are using an architect for the building contract, he or she will take care of employing the right people for you. The architect will know experienced builders and craftspeople in your area and will invite some of them to quote for the job. Once you have settled on one, the architect will write a repair specification, which the builder must follow to the letter, and will also decide whether or not you need approval for any of the jobs.

If the work to be done is substantial and you decide to employ a builder, as well as any specialists, make sure you draw up a good, clear contract with the builder. It should detail the full extent of the work in advance, which will help avoid adding extras later. Extras can be expensive and prevent the builder from completing the work – because the builder has commitments elsewhere, for example. The Joint Contracts Tribunal (JCT) produces a standard building contract that you can use.

To save money and keep an eye on work, many owner-restorers like to work on site. Doing much of the labouring yourself while leaving the complex jobs to specialists can save money, but is time-consuming, back-breaking work – hard to fit in if you also have a full-time job. Alternatively, you may even decide to project manage the work yourself. This involves opening up the site each day, drawing up a schedule of works and a budget, ensuring materials are ordered and arrive when needed and that all contractors and suppliers are paid. You need to run the build like a military operation, but also have the right personality to get on with everyone working on the project. A happy team means you are more likely to achieve good results on time.

Project managing is a major responsibility. If you are committed to another full-time job, then you probably cannot spare the time to be on site. Be realistic about what you can take on and don't be deterred from using a professional project manager because of the fee. Project managers charge around 10% of the cost of the project, but you could waste that amount or more on over-running schedules and unnecessary mistakes.

Depending on the house's condition and your financial state, you may have to treat your restoration as a long-term project to spread the costs. Many owners find it is the only approach to take – they simply cannot afford to tackle everything in one go. Initially, you should carry out essential repairs to ensure the building is watertight. Repair the roof, check gutters and downpipes are not blocked and maintain exterior paintwork. Then organise the restoration work in blocks, as you can afford it. This system allows you to get to know your house thoroughly and make the best decisions. You also have time to build up contacts with good local tradesmen and craftspeople.

The other route to take is that chosen by the die-hard restorer: doing everything yourself, from labouring to decorating.

This takes time, experience and lots of hard work. The help of friends or relatives, especially with labouring, can be invaluable, but do not rely on them to step forward when you need them or stick to promises of assistance.

It is possible – but not easy – to take on this kind of project while still holding down a day job. You must be realistic about deadlines – the work won't get done as quickly as if you were there full time – and be prepared to work every weekend and spare hour for many months.

You will also have to read up extensively to fill gaps in your knowledge and attend courses to learn skills specific to your kind of house – how to mix and work with lime plaster, for example. These offer the chance to speak to and learn from an expert, which can be invaluable. The SPAB runs courses through the year all over Britain and many local colleges and institutions also offer short courses. It's worth checking with specialist suppliers, too, many of whom run introductory courses in using the materials they supply. Doing all the work yourself is not for the faint hearted, but satisfaction and pride in a house that you personally restored are the ultimate rewards.

Look before you leap

With any restoration work, there are basic logistics to consider. First of all, where will you live while the work is being carried out? Even if the house you are restoring is in a poor state, you may choose to live in it. Although potentially uncomfortable, there are benefits. With a large project, for example, even just doing an hour a day can make a big difference and, if you are on site, it's easier to fit in this valuable extra time.

Living in the property also means that the house and any materials being stored in and around it are safer. Remember, though, that this is not an easy option, and if you feel that by living in the house you might actually slow down the work and frustrate builders, it will probably work out cheaper to live elsewhere.

You could rent a house or flat while work proceeds. Choose one as close to the site as possible. Even if you are taking a hands-off approach to the work, you will still need to make numerous site visits to check progress and consult with builders, so proximity is essential. For large projects taking several months, it might be cheaper to buy a static caravan (for around £6,000) and park it on site than to pay rent. You may need permission from your local planning office to do this – check first.

Think about insurance. You will need comprehensive and often complex insurance cover from a specialist when restoring a wreck, which can prove expensive. Specialist insurers like Chubb or

Hiscox will look closely at the date of all parts of the building and its features and will ask you to complete a questionnaire providing details of the contractor, their public liability cover, their insurers and limit of indemnity, plus a full description of works to be carried out. Insurers will also need to know the contract value, contract period, details of security at the site and fire protection during the works. If your property will be uninhabited during the works, extra theft cover may be needed. It all adds up.

Security is another issue. If the house is empty or is easily accessible via scaffolding, open doorways or fallen fences, check that this does not invalidate your insurance. There is a thriving market for stolen items today and original features are often snatched from empty homes. Fireplaces, panelling, doors and handles, glass panels, light switches, paving, roof slates and ironmongery sell quickly on the black market. A Victorian terrace may be even more at risk than a grand listed building: features in architecturally important homes are often photographed and inventoried, making them harder to sell, but a cast-iron fireplace or set of doors taken from a standard 19th-century property are almost impossible to trace back to their original home. Even building materials can disappear from gardens when left stacked overnight, so be vigilant.

It is a good idea to photograph everything inside and outside the house so that you can reclaim property or find appropriate substitutes if anything does get stolen. Take pictures of fireplaces, mouldings, panelling, original features like old ovens or fire grates, and even small details like latches or bell pushes. Outside, photograph any paving, ironwork, statuary and even the roof tiles. It doesn't take long and adds an extra, useful layer of security. During the day, it can be difficult to tell legitimate workers from thieves when workmen and vehicles are coming and going, so don't be afraid to challenge people on site or even request that they wear ID.

Finally, when work does start, make sure that all interior features are protected thoroughly. Even the most careful and conscientious builder can have an accident and details like floorboards or tiled floors can be quickly ruined by countless workmen's shoes tramping over them.

Take photos of small details like latches, in case they are stolen or damaged while restoration work is underway.

Masterminding a long-term project

Set in beautiful gardens in west Suffolk, the grade II listed thatched farmhouse that belongs to Widget Finn and husband Tim dates back to the 16th century. Over 13 years, the couple has undertaken three phases of work to restore the property's character while at the same time introducing a few modern comforts.

What did the three stages of work involve? First, we did essentials. We rewired and tore out a lot of the plasterboard that was put up in the 1950s to hide the beams and fireplaces. Then we ran out of money. Four years later we started again, moving the staircase so it came into the hall not the dining room, installing a bathroom upstairs to replace the one in the lean-to and putting in central heating. The last phase, recently completed, was converting what was the cheese loft above the dairy (now the kitchen) into two bedrooms and a bathroom.

Did you expect the work to take this long? No. It's always the same with old buildings; you live in hope that it will be done quickly. It was six years before we had central heating — we just couldn't afford it.

How did you find good craftspeople? We were very lucky because our builder put us in contact with them all — the thatcher, the ironworker who made the latches and hinges, and a few others. The best recommendation is someone that your builder uses.

Did you have to get permission for work? Yes. We initially submitted a schedule of work to our local conservation officer, but as is inevitable with old buildings, as you go along you find things that need further approval. We uncovered three fireplaces in one hearth, for example. The 1950s yellow tiled one, then a Victorian one and eventually the original inglenook. The conservation officer would pop over and advise us each time a new discovery was made.

Restoration work on old properties like this farmhouse can take several years.

Choosing the right materials

The materials used in rural properties, especially those more than 150 years old, can be quite different from those used in city buildings. You don't, for instance, find many thatched roofs in towns. In general, any property that predates the industrial revolution of the mid-19th century will have been built with softer, more breathable materials than the mass-produced bricks, tiles and paint used today.

More porous bricks, breathable lime-based renders and plasters, stone or even earth were all used to construct and cover walls. These materials gave old houses a degree of flexibility and breathability that should not be interfered with and that cannot be replicated by modern impermeable cements, bricks and paint.

As well as the building techniques of its time, a house might have been constructed in a vernacular tradition using specific local materials and methods. The spread of the railways during the industrial revolution made it easier and cheaper to transport materials across the country, but before that, it was cheaper to use local materials, so a building's roofing, flooring and walls will all tell a local story. In Lincolnshire, for example, earth-walled houses were made using a local technique called mud and stud, which is part earth and part timber frame and unique to the region. In areas of the southeast, the practice of using locally found flint in walls has given the region's buildings and walls a distinctive character.

When restoring a rural property, you will come across a range of interesting historic materials, from square quarry tiles to brick paviours, to thatch, handmade clay tiles or Welsh slate. Becoming familiar with them, understanding why they were used and finding out where to source authentic replacements is essential to a successful restoration.

A decorative wall frieze created using the traditional technique of pargetting.

Reclaimed versus new

Using modern materials in a period property is generally considered bad practice. An old building should read as an old building, with synthetic materials used only as an exception. They have no sympathy with the property's shape and size and, in the case of impermeable materials like cement, can actually damage its fabric.

Modern bricks, cement and even paint are hard and impervious. They make a building watertight, trapping in moisture that can then damage its structure. The traditional renders, plasters and paint used on old buildings allowed them to breathe – moisture soaked in and then evaporated off the building all the time. To prevent this process is to harm the building.

The Society for the Protection of Ancient Buildings (SPAB) advocates the use of new materials made with traditional skills. Using a company that can supply handmade bricks to match originals is not only good for your home, but for regional enterprise, too. Sourcing traditional materials like stone has led to the reopening of many local quarries, like the sandstone quarries in Herefordshire. Such initiatives deserve support.

Many advisory bodies discourage the use of salvaged materials, because of the increase in theft and inappropriate stripping of buildings to supply this lucrative market. The trade in stolen architectural salvage is estimated to be worth more than £300 million a year. However, if honestly sourced, salvaged pieces can enjoy a reincarnation in a sympathetic home – much better than being scrapped and lost – and provide authentic period detail. If you do buy from a salvage yard, make sure it subscribes to the Salvo code (see chapter nine for more information). This guarantees that items were not removed from a protected building without permission.

Aim to use materials salvaged from your own building, too. Repair – rather than replace – and recycle is the best advice.

The fabric of the building

Roof coverings

Natural slate and stone

Slate is a tough and relatively maintenance-free roof covering, associated particularly with Scotland, Wales, Cornwall and Cumbria – smooth blue-grey slate from Wales is perhaps the best-known variety. After the industrial revolution, it became possible to transport slate easily, so today it crops up on buildings all over the country.

If you have slates missing, take a sample along to a roofing material supplier to get a good match. The slate should be the same colour, size and thickness and, where possible, from the same source. Where total re-slating is needed (on roofs where around one fifth of the slate has already been repaired and repairs are no longer cost effective), try to salvage any reusable slates from the existing structure. The trade in salvaged slates has led to the unnecessary destruction of roofs, so buying reclaimed slate is not always a good idea. If you do buy slates from a salvage yard, make sure it is one that subscribes to the Salvo code (see chapter nine), which ensures that materials sold are honestly sourced.

Stone slates (tiles cut from stone rather than slate) are similar to slate and should be treated the same way. They are also durable, lasting for hundreds of years, and reusable.

Clay tiles

Until labour-saving mechanisation was introduced in the 19th century, roof tiles were made by hand to a standard size – established by Edward IV in the 15th century and changed little since. Early handmade tiles were not completely flat, but had a cross camber, from head to tail and side to side, to provide ventilation as well as protection from rainwater. Bear this in mind when trying to match tiles: modern versions often don't have this curved shape.

Thatch

Regional building traditions will dictate which type of thatch a building has – either long straw, combed wheat or water reed. As thatching demands a high degree of skill, any work should always be carried out by a local thatcher using, ideally, local materials. If your property is listed, any changes to the design and character of the thatch may need listed building consent.

External walls

Timber framework

Structural timber in walls, floors and roofs can last indefinitely if properly maintained: houses built with a structural wooden framework are among the oldest still in use. The familiar half-timbered house is made from a stout oak framework infilled with bricks or lightweight wattle and daub. As well as oak, chestnut and other hard woods were typically used and grow incredibly hard with age, sometimes capable of blunting or breaking modern metal blades. The timber was often unseasoned or 'green', which can lead to distortion as the wood naturally moves and hardens.

Brick

From the late 17th century, brick became Britain's principal building material. It became vital in areas where stone doesn't occur naturally. It's cheap, convenient to use, fire resistant and all but the softest brickwork lasts indefinitely, provided the pointing is sound. Bricks were produced locally during the Georgian period and often on site, with the colour varying according to the local earths used. Today, many companies offer handmade traditional-style bricks to match those existing in a building. Expect to pay around £1 a brick (plus VAT).

Stone

Stone has been used for centuries to build every kind of house, from simple cottages to grand manors. It was more expensive than brick and generally considered more prestigious.

There are many regional varieties. In the southwest the local Bath stone, a limestone, has been used since Roman times and in particular in the 18th and 19th centuries when John Wood and Beau Nash used it to develop the classic Georgian architecture of Bath. It has a mellow, sandy colour. Portland stone, quarried in Dorset since the 12th century, is a grey limestone. It is durable, high quality and was typically used around the south. Cotswold stone is quarried near Cheltenham and has been used locally for centuries, while in parts of Scotland granite is the local building material – Aberdeen is known as the granite city.

The most expensive form of stone was ashlar – smoothly finished blocks that fitted neatly together. Often, ashlar was used only as a veneer for facing a building and rough stone, rubble or brick would have been used behind it.

Flint

Flint has been used for all sorts of buildings since ancient times, particularly in the south and east of England where it occurs naturally. Flint is very hard and impervious. Typically it is used in thick, rubble-cored walls and often the flint was knapped – split to achieve a deliberate aesthetic effect. The most common problems with flint-walled properties is the tendency for the flint to loosen and fall out. If there is a lot of flint missing from your property's walls and you are worried about stability, seek the advice of a structural engineer.

Render

Most traditional renders were made with lime and were soft compared with modern cement-based wall coverings. Traditional renders were absorbent and allowed rainwater to soak in, then dry out again naturally. They were also flexible, allowing for movement in the walls without cracking. External renders were deliberately 'sacrificial' – that is, they would ultimately decay, but were cheaper and easier to replace than the walls they covered.

Render can be quite rough, incorporating pebbles or small stones, or beautifully smooth. The coarsest render is called roughcast, which contains fairly big stones and was applied by being thrown at the wall. The smoothest finish is stucco, which was often marked or 'lined out' to imitate stonework.

Lime renders need repainting every five to eight years with a traditional final coating

of limewash, which allows the building to breath. Limewash is still readily available and can be bought ready mixed, costing around £14 per litre. It should be used instead of modern impermeable paints.

Ironwork

Wrought iron was used to make railings, balconies and gates for some of our most handsome buildings, but iron was also less glamorously used for gutters and downpipes. Rust is its biggest enemy and both cast and wrought iron need regular painting to protect them, ideally every few years.

Flooring

Solid floors

Solid floors are found at basement and ground-floor level. Early floors were no more than earth, rammed down to make it hard and flat, often with ashes and ox blood added to bond the mix. Later, solid floors were simply laid over an earth floor on a bed of ash or sand. A range of materials was used, from stone flags to the patterned ceramic tiles that were first popular in medieval times. Typically, solid floors were found in a property's utilitarian areas – the kitchens, workshops and cellars – but the idea spread, and affluent home owners began using

Solid stone floors are typically found in kitchens and other utilitarian areas.

marble slabs or coloured stone for halls and passageways. Paved floors were at first a luxury only the wealthy could afford, until the late 17th century when a greater affluence and the availability of cheaper materials meant they were adopted by all strata of society.

Tiles became widely used in the 1850s, with the invention of the encaustic tile in 1840. This was made by inlaying different coloured clays that fused together when fired. Such was the Victorians' passion for them that by the late 1870s, these tiles were being used in halls right up to the dado rail. They were also used in conservatories, hearths and grates and, later, in bathrooms.

Suspended floors

These are laid over timber beams or joists and were generally made of wood, although in some 19th-century and earlier houses they were made of plaster laid on reeds or laths. Early timber floorboards were typically much wider than those found in a Victorian house and were often made of hardwoods such as oak or elm. It wasn't until the 17th century that softwood boards, like pine, began to be widely used.

Internal joinery

As well as doors, door frames, skirting boards and window frames, a period property may have more elaborate internal joinery – a handsome oak staircase with a finely carved newel post or beautiful wall panelling. Hardwood like oak was used for internal joinery until the late 17th century, when softwoods like pine became widely available. Softwood joinery was almost always painted or grained to imitate hardwood.

Interior panelling has a long tradition. Oak panelling was always used in larger houses of the 16th and 17th centuries, but by the late 17th century, softwood panelling became widespread and fashionable until the mid-18th century. The Georgians typically panelled below the dado rail in deal or pine, painting it in a light colour such as stone. Softwood timber was grown more slowly than it is today, so it was harder and more durable, which explains why you can still find examples of Georgian softwood panelling in excellent condition. The Edwardian era saw a revival of Georgian-style panelling, a light-coloured alternative to the more heavy, dark wooden panelling beloved of the Tudors. It was painted white or clean pale colours.

Internal wall coverings

Plaster and render

Traditional plasters and renders were usually a mix of lime, sand and animal hair (often horse hair), although earth or clay-

Features like the wooden floorboards of this former granary are still beautiful today.

114

based plaster can be found. They would have been applied directly to a solid wall, or onto the timber laths of partition walls or ceilings. Lime plaster had a typically plain finish, but in high-status buildings was sometimes decorative. From the 16th to the 18th century, decorative plaster mouldings would have been handmade. By the late 18th century, gypsum and plaster of Paris became widely used, so decorative plasterwork could be precast in moulds. Mass-produced fibrous plaster was introduced in the 19th century, so the walls in many Victorian properties were finished with this. It has a smooth finish.

Paint

Distemper and limewash were typically used to paint internal walls. At its simplest, limewash is made by adding water to lime putty, a material derived from burnt limestone. Natural pigments were sometimes added to colour the paint, including yellow ochre or animal blood. Limewash doesn't produce the uniform coverage or colour we expect from modern emulsions, but its tonal variations and soft texture are part of its charm. It needs frequent reapplication, every few years.

Distemper also has a soft texture and can be pigmented more strongly than limewash. It's made from a mixture of crushed chalk and glue. Sometimes linseed oil was added to toughen it and improve durability.

In Georgian times (1760–1830), interiors were as colourful as the materials available allowed them to be. Pastel blues and greens were commonly used on newly plastered walls, made by mixing copper or iron sulphate into the plaster to deter mildew. A passion for these pastel shades persisted long after their practical origin had been forgotten.

If you find any original paintwork in your home, paint scrapes can be taken for analysis. The results may not be completely accurate, as colours may have faded over time, but they will give an impression of the historic colours used in the house and help you to source similar shades.

Oil paints made using lead were generally used on joinery and metalwork inside and out. As lead is potentially hazardous, lead paint is now only available for use on grade I and II* buildings in England. Check the resources section in chapter nine for specialists who can supply it.

Wallpaper

Examples of wallpaper survive from as early as the 16th century, but it became really popular from the mid-18th century, when it was used as a substitute for wall hangings or plaster decoration. Georgian wallpapers typically included delicate hand-painted scenes, wood-block prints or flock papers made to look like wall hangings, while in the Regency period of the early 19th century, stripes were very popular.

Up until the 1840s, wallpaper was printed by hand using wood blocks, which was time consuming and expensive. When the process became fully mechanised, large-scale production was possible. Wallpaper became cheaper and everybody wanted it. By the mid-1800s, an interiors-conscious Victorian could buy papers in bright colours, thanks to the development of new dyes, while flock wallpapers and papers with raised decoration, such as Lincrusta, were also available and the height of fashion.

Early wallpaper is sometimes discovered in cupboards or behind fitted furniture. Light,

humidity, damp and movement in the wall can all damage it, but a specialist conservator may be able to repair fragile old wallpaper without removing it from the walls. If you want to create a period feel, seek out one of the many companies that produce replicas of archive wallpaper patterns.

Cole & Son has a vast archive of traditional patterns and can make wallpaper using age-old techniques like block printing by hand. It holds over 4,000 hand-carved wooden blocks associated with key designers like William Morris and Augustus Pugin. Another company that supplies historical print papers is GP & J Baker.

Introducing home comforts

While you might be able to give your cottage back its 16th-century charm, or restore your 1860s terrace to its Victorian best, you will also want your home to operate with some degree of 21st-century comfort and practicality. Electricity, hot water and some form of heating are on most people's list of essentials, but installing these mod cons requires sensitivity. Here are some tips.

Electricity

Connecting to the mains

If your house isn't connected to mains electricity, contact the local planning department or power supplier about the feasibility of getting connected. Generally, it is possible, except in specific locations – for example, National Parks.

If you can't be connected, using a generator is the alternative. They run on diesel, petrol or liquefied petroleum gas (LPG) and can power everything in your home, including sensitive equipment like computers. Just Generators can supply you with a suitable generator, based on your total wattage requirements (see chapter nine for contact details).

Rewiring

Early electrical wiring is nearly always unsafe by modern standards, so old properties usually need rewiring. It's a complex job. New electrical installations should minimise damage to the building's historic fabric and be unobtrusive, but at the same time be legal and safe. There needs to be a balance between respecting the building's historical character and installing an efficient power supply. You should also think beyond the initial rewiring and keep in mind the subsequent use, maintenance and testing of the installation – will you damage floorboards or panelling each time you need to access it?

Rather than just employing any electrician from the Yellow Pages, contact the National Inspection Council for Electrical Installation Contracting (NICEIC) to find an experienced electrical engineer who has worked on a similar building to yours.

The SPAB recommends that, if possible, you get a qualified electrical engineer involved early in a restoration project so that he or she can work with architects and surveyors to consider all aspects – technical, aesthetic and practical. Its *Technical Pamphlet 9 – Electrical Installations* is very helpful. English Heritage's leaflet *Investigative Work on Historic Buildings* is a useful guide covering the opening-up stage of projects.

You can sometimes refurbish and reuse decorative switches, while old conduits and gas pipework can be used for new cabling, to save damaging walls. If you do have to pull up floorboards or remove panelling, employ a specialist joiner to do it in order to minimise damage – rather than just heaving them up yourself.

Gas

In a property without mains gas, LPG can be used in exactly the same way, for heating, cooking and hot water. Storage tanks can be installed above or below ground and Calor's new Think Tank automatically orders gas when your supply is low. Set-up costs for Calor LPG in the first year are competitive: tank installation and the cost of the boiler itself are both less than for oil (LPG boilers cost around £1,200; oil, £2,400).

Oil

Its reasonable running costs make oil another popular fuel. It costs about 17p per litre; the average cost of space and water heating for a three-bedroom house is around £470 per year. Tanks are an eyesore, so consider where to site yours. There is no maximum distance from your property, so you could hide it in an outbuilding. Just make sure it's accessible to the tanker for refilling. Tanker hoses are typically 25 metres long maximum, but check with your oil supplier. For comprehensive information, look at the Oil Firing Technical Association (OFTEC) website or call its technical advice line.

Agas and Rayburns

Agas run on natural or propane gas, oil or electricity, but are used only for cooking. They will also gently warm the room they are sited in. Rayburn Heatrangers run on oil, natural gas, LPG, smokeless fuel, wood and peat briquettes and can be used for cooking, hot water and central heating, assuming your property isn't huge. They will happily run between 12 and 20 radiators; if your house has more, seek the advice of a heating engineer about what size or combination of appliances you will need.

Radiators

Radiators should never be hung on wood-panelled walls as they will put great strain on them. Instead, use free-standing traditional low cast-iron radiators. Even radiators situated near panelling or woodwork can dry it out and shrink it if the heat is on high for too long, so try to keep temperatures reasonably low and constant.

Underfloor heating

Modern underfloor heating is invisible and unobtrusive. Installing it is disruptive, though (the existing floor must be lifted), and it operates at low temperatures (a problem in a draughty, thermally inefficient old property), so many suppliers won't fit it in a period home. If, however, you are converting a property, you may be able to use it, as you can lay it at build stage before you put a new floor on top, as well as ensuring the building has the right degree of insulation to make underfloor heating functional.

Broadband

If you want broadband or extra phone lines, think about installing additional sockets and cabling at the build stage, so they are as unobtrusive as possible and you do not have to disrupt the building at a later date to fit them. Since summer 2005, BT has delivered connection to broadband accross the whole country.

Insulation

Roof insulation is generally straightforward to install in a period home and a good way to improve its thermal efficiency and keep fuel bills down. Quality environmentally friendly insulators are now available; for example, Thermafleece made from British sheep's wool, and cellulose insulation made from recycled paper. Remember, though, that adding insulation to any roof can bring with it unexpected problems like damp or mould growth, encouraged by the warm conditions. Sufficient ventilation once the insulation is laid should prevent this; ask your installer to check.

Eco-friendly alternatives

There are numerous green alternatives to traditional methods of heating and powering our homes, and installing them need not be more expensive, either – grants are available for green improvements to your property under the government's Clear Skies initiative. The only drawback is that many green heating and power systems involve altering the appearance of a house's exterior, which can be problematical with protected period properties. Discuss any plans for eco-friendly installations with your conservation officer first, but here's a rough outline of what you might, or might not, be able to use.

Eco power

Solar

Solar power is the process of harnessing the sun's energy to create electricity or heat water. Solar water heaters collect the heat in vacuum tubes or via an absorbing metal plate. The heat is taken via by a liquid medium (water or oil) to a heat exchanger, usually inside a hot water cylinder. To make electricity, photovoltaic cells, which convert light energy to electrical energy, are used. The British climate and tendency to overcast skies make both systems unreliable, but they can be used in conjunction with conventional power sources to boost efficiency.

If your property is listed, in a conservation area or National Park, you'll need consent to install a solar hot water system with roof panels and, in reality, are unlikely to get it. It's also not feasible to fix solar panels to thatch. An alternative is installing panels on frames in the grounds, but if this spoils the appearance of the property, it too is likely to get the thumbs down from a planning officer.

Wind turbines

Wind energy is almost certainly the most effective way of generating renewable energy in Britain, especially since in mid-winter, when demand for power and heat is at its highest, the amount of energy that can be harvested from the sun is almost zero.

To generate electricity from wind turbines, you must live in an area that gets plenty of wind and where turbines are permitted to be erected. Many protected areas, including Areas of Outstanding Natural Beauty (AONBs), don't allow them. They need to be as high as possible and away from obstructions like buildings or trees that interfere with their efficiency, so you will need quite a lot of land to install one. Once permission has been granted, your site needs to be monitored to establish feasibility. This takes around six months of metering the wind, to see if there is enough to generate sufficient power, so installation is never immediate.

Micro hydro systems

If you have a fast-flowing stream on your property, you may be able to generate power from it with a micro hydro system, typically used by owners of converted watermills. These systems harness the energy of the passing water to generate electricity. They are effective and economical, often producing more power than your property needs, so you may then be able to sell some back to the National Grid. In reality, though, few properties have the right conditions and water flow to install one.

Eco heating

Wood-burning boilers

These burn logs, wood chips or pellets for central heating. They create less pollution than fossil fuels and use a sustainable resource. Feeding your boiler with scrap wood or wood from renewable coppicing is the greenest option. Grants for installing approved wood-burning products are available under the government's Clear Skies initiative.

Ground-source heat pumps

They absorb heat from the top few metres of soil, using pipes buried in the earth, which is then used to warm your house. The advantage is that it's a discrete system, but it operates at low temperatures so it is not ideal in a draughty, thermally inefficient house. It's also best used with underfloor heating (see above), which often cannot be installed in an old house.

Further reading

The SPAB sells a range of titles covering all aspects of restoring and caring for historic buildings, including *House and Cottage Restoration – Do's and Don'ts* by Hugh Lander (£10.95 plus £1.30 p&p) and *Old House Care and Repair* by Janet Collings (Donhead, £25 plus £3.20 p&p).

Wood-burning stoves and boilers can be more ecologically sound and fuel-efficient than other forms of heating.

CHAPTER SEVEN

Clever conversions

From barns to stations, churches to cowsheds, there is something incredibly romantic about living in a converted building. The uniqueness, beauty and historical importance of most converted properties make them easy to fall in love with. Barns, the most commonly converted buildings, typically boast lofty ceilings and plenty of open-plan space, while a converted chapel may still have its original stained glass or carved wooden joinery.

Buying a converted property is one thing; converting one yourself is quite another. These buildings were never intended as domestic dwellings, so turning them into homes requires skill and imagination. Barns, churches, mews and any of the myriad buildings transformed into homes today were built as practical, hard-working structures. They were places to meet, store crops or house animals or machinery and their layouts reflect this. Those people who successfully pull off a conversion share a sympathetic feeling for the building and its fabric, and an ability to look beyond its often bare appearance – without power, plastered walls or plumbing – to imagine a finished, comfortable home. Together with this vision, they have plenty of energy and resourcefulness to cope with the frustrations and problems, both administrative and structural, that inevitably crop up during a project.

Conversions can be costly, time consuming and tough to get past planners. Even when consent is granted, it may come with a string of restrictions that might interfere with your initial ideas. This chapter sets out the key considerations of converting, with specific advice for those interested in transforming a barn or church.

Converting a property – the key issues

Converted buildings score high on interest and appeal, but the living space they create can be flawed. Even the smartest architect will not be able to make them flow as well or work as ergonomically as a straightforward house and there is not always an elegant design solution to the problems they pose.

The layout and appearance of the building will be subject to planning restrictions, so you need to have a flexible approach and be prepared to make compromises. Work with what you have and do not try to impose a specific design on a quirky, historical building. Instead, think about how you can build on its best features to compensate for the odd negative thrown up by its unusual proportions. There may be nooks or crannies created by the design of the building that seem like wasted space, but putting up shelves or installing built-in furniture makes better use of them than trying to conceal them.

Storage is often compromised, too. A chapel or barn conversion may not have attic space to store your clutter, but you will have lofty ceilings or beautiful beams that more than make up for this. Think about where you can build in storage elsewhere, perhaps at ground floor level, and talk to the architect about this.

Converting a building is always costly. Good conversions require careful design

and planning, plus sensitive building work, much of which may need to be done by hand and all of which are expensive. You will often need to use handmade, traditional materials, too, and these can cost a great deal more than their modern, off-the-shelf equivalents. However, a well-converted building will repay you many times over by being both a beautiful and a well-planned place in which to live and one that is unique.

Planning consent is another important factor to consider. The planning process will take at the very least three months and, as no vendor is likely to be happy to wait that long before you can make an offer, it's important to get advice from an architect or surveyor who has experience of similar conversion projects in the same area straightaway. He or she will have an idea of local planning authority policy – what types of conversions they will accept and what they will reject. This will help you decide whether you want to make an offer or not. To find a surveyor or architect familiar with converting the type of building you are interested in buying, ask the estate agent or visit owners of other recently converted properties nearby and find out who they used.

Planning policy for conversions is fairly consistent throughout Britain. The basic stance is simple – it makes sense to reuse rural buildings and, while it might be preferable to convert them for commercial or economic use, making them into homes is also acceptable. There are regional exceptions, though. In East Northants, you cannot convert an agricultural building unless it is going to be lived in by an agricultural worker. The Yorkshire Dales Park Authority is considering plans to allow conversions only if they will be lived in by local people who need to live and work in the park, particularly key workers. Some local authorities only allow you to convert barns if they will be used as holiday homes.

When plans are accepted, it may be with certain restrictions; planning officials are eager to maintain the integrity and appearance of old buildings. New doors or chimneys can be areas of contention, and any degree of demolition is unacceptable. You might think you can knock down most of the structure and start again, or just replace a wall or two, but you are unlikely to get consent for this. Your plans need to be able to demonstrate that the building can be converted without substantial rebuilding.

The planned conversion must not change the building's surroundings dramatically: for example, creating car parking space will alter the land around the building. Installing mains water, power or sewerage with all the necessary pipework and cabling visible on the outside walls can detract from its appearance and planners will frown on this.

Accessibility is often an issue and, in remote areas, getting permission to lay a road up to the property may be impossible. This is why many remote barns and farm buildings remain unconverted even though in theory they could make wonderfully private and unique homes.

Unlike some restoration projects, it is generally not a good idea to try to live in a building that you are converting while work is taking place. When restoring a house, if you are lucky there are one or two habitable rooms and some basic services to make it just about possible, but an old cowshed, derelict barn or watermill full of its original machinery will offer no such luxuries. Attempting to camp out – literally – is enough to break the spirit of all but the keenest convertors so look into other options. It is advisable to live near the site, though. This makes it much easier to work on the project or just check whether it is progressing according to plan.

Even if you have experience of restoration projects on other houses, it may still be advisable to use a project manager for a conversion. Conversions throw up challenges and problems not found when working on a conventional house and a project manager or an architect who can also project manage will ensure that no corners are cut, problems are dealt with quickly and work finishes on schedule.

Look into the VAT situation. As with building a new house, significantly changing an existing building means you do not have to pay VAT on the work and materials. On this basis you might assume that conversions are VAT exempt, but that is not always the case. It varies from project to project, and even experienced architects can struggle to say whether VAT is payable on a particular conversion and, if so, how much. To find out for sure, contact your local VAT office. If no VAT is payable, this just means that your builder will leave it off his bill. Materials should then also be VAT exempt, although it can be tricky to explain this to the cashier at your local builder's merchants. You will still pay VAT on professional fees – your architect's or surveyor's bills.

Converting a building not originally intended for domestic habitation is a great way to create a unique home.

What the local planning authority will expect

Your local authority planning office will have a set of considerations that apply to any application to convert an old building. Some are obvious, but some cover issues you may not have considered. Here's a rough outline of the chief concerns.

First, it is very important that the conversion should respect and retain the character of the original building. The general appearance should be simple and uncluttered. Your planning authority will not like work that tries to over-domesticate or 'prettify' a building.

The planning authority will specify use of good-quality natural materials, sourced locally if possible. You will be expected to respect the original storey heights: an obviously single-storey building should not be converted into two storeys by raising the roof. Extensions are generally forbidden, too, as they undermine the intrinsic character of the building.

When it comes to the interior layout, aim to retain the original structure, windows, doors and features with as few changes as possible. And if you think you'd like to create a first floor inside your lofty barn, you might have to think again. Adding floors may not be appropriate in large buildings like barns and chapels, especially if they are listed.

Roofs are subject to several restrictions. Putting in a domestic chimney stack is almost always unsuitable and over-restoring the roof is a no-no. It should not look new, so you should preserve the existing structure and will be expected to match replacement tiles to the originals.

If your property is listed, it will be subject to even tougher restrictions. In fact, conversion may not be permitted at all. The countryside would lose a great deal of its architectural heritage, after all, if every barn was converted for domestic use. Where conversions are permitted to listed buildings, alterations are expected to respect the existing internal and external features, including floor beams, date stones and external stairs.

You may also be restricted by wildlife. Farm buildings have traditionally been the home of a range of species, many of which are now protected. It is an offence to destroy or obstruct the roosts of bats and barn owls, and you must inform English Nature if you intend to work on a building used by either.

Churches and barns

Two of the most commonly converted building types in this country are churches and barns. Both offer generous living space with plenty of character, but both also present their own set of challenges to the would-be convertor.

Chief among these is the issue of windows. Farm buildings generally have few door and window openings compared to the overall area of wall. As they were used primarily for storage, there was no need for regular windows to let in light. Nevertheless, the style and type of openings that they do have are important features, varying from large arched openings for carts to small slit vents and pigeon holes. Churches, on the other hand, often have an abundance of windows, which are usually tall, characteristically styled and set high in the walls. If you are planning to convert a barn or church, tampering with existing windows or adding new ones can spoil its appearance. New windows should be added sparingly and in a way that maintains the original mass of the building.

Where you do add new openings, it is generally necessary for the window and door joinery to be purpose-made for the building, to conserve its original character. This can be expensive. You are unlikely to get permission to add modern-style windows that are too domestic in character for a barn or church conversion.

Converting barns into dwellings has been popular for many years now, which means all the best and most obviously convertible barns have probably already been snapped up. If you do find one in its original state, it's likely to pose some tough challenges and need a lot of work, or it would probably have been converted already.

Chapels and churches often come with features like pulpits and fonts that you have to work around. Just as barns have high ceilings and beams that can be hard to incorporate, so these religious features can challenge even the most inventive architect and may end up looking awkward and out of place.

The shape and size of churches also make them tricky to turn into ideal homes. Small, boxy chapels that have just one main hall and tall windows can be the hardest to make into homes: their dimensions limit design possibilities and make them expensive to heat. Once converted, they can look rather out of proportion.

An energy-efficient barn conversion

Jonathan Williams, an engineer, and his wife Sharon spent two years converting their 19th-century barn near Salisbury. Using the latest green technology, they have created an energy efficient, environmentally-friendly home that runs purely on electricity and is extremely cost effective.

How did you find the barn? Through an estate agent. He didn't think we would be interested, but its lovely views and the fact that it came with quite a bit of land made it unmissable. We had looked at building plots with the idea of building a home from scratch, but they were always pocket-handkerchief sized.

Were you daunted by the project? Just a little. Barns are notoriously difficult to convert and can be incredibly expensive to do. They often need a lot of work done by hand and you can't use standard-size materials, so that makes them costly. This place needed an enormous amount of work. It was about to collapse, had a corrugated iron roof and was surrounded by waist-high nettles.

Why did you decide to give the conversion a green angle? It just seemed a good opportunity to try something new. Once we had chosen to have a ground-source heat pump [see chapter six] to provide our heating, it dictated that we use a number of other green additions, like good-quality

insulation. We used warm cell insulation made from recycled newspaper, to make the building as energy efficient as possible.

What have been the chief benefits of going green? A ground-source heat pump used with underfloor heating produces gentle warmth. Rather than having rapidly fluctuating temperatures like in a modern house, where you flick the heating on and it's warm in 10 minutes, it's a very constant environment. The real advantage is you can operate the heat pumps at night when electricity is cheaper, but because the house is well built and insulated the temperature remains steady. Some people argue it's a waste keeping it warm during the day if you're out, but there isn't a significant amount of waste. Another bonus is that there are no clunking pipes, no radiators and the constant environment means there's a feeling of stillness. We all feel healthier.

Was it difficult to get planning permission for your ideas? The barn already had outline consent for conversion to a dwelling when we bought it. The architect took care of getting our plans approved and it was pretty straightforward. In the end we found that, provided we put forward sensible ideas and were prepared to compromise, there wasn't a problem. For example, we had discussions with the planning officer about what type of brickwork we would use at the base of the barn. They wanted us to use an English bond type, but it wouldn't have been suitable for a cavity wall – and we needed a cavity wall in order to satisfy building regs. So we said, if we can use the bricks we want, how about we use handmade tiles on the roof. The planning officers are looking for an overall effect, so a degree of trading can take place to get the right balance.

How did you manage the work?

An architect did the drawings and calculations. I managed the construction. I worked with a contractor who had a team of builders and plasterers. I would go to the site in the morning, check everyone knew what to do that day, then go to work and order what was needed. In the later stages of the build, I did all the electrical installation, too. I often worked weekends. It was pretty exhausting.

Any major problems? We wanted to retain the character of the building as far as we could and had to keep the original structural members. This involved careful thought and some compromises: like adapting the shape of the stairs to fit around the arrangement of internal beams. The roof structure is A-frames. The upstairs rooms had to be arranged between the A-frames, and we needed stairs that could get to all the rooms. There are stairs serving either end of the barn, but one set forks at the top into two sections, one going one side of the A-frame and one going the other.

The ground was the biggest problem. The barn was just resting on the earth, typical of old agricultural buildings of two centuries ago. We had to put in proper foundations and, when we started work, we found that the ground condition was atrocious. It just was not strong enough to support the building. Work stopped for two months while we planned what to do and drew up new designs. We came up with a raft foundation, which is much more expensive and has a complicated construction, and then had to get it approved by building regulations.

What does it cost to run the barn? The pumps are powered by electricity and we don't need any other fuels. Our total bill for heating, lighting, hot water – everything – is about £600 a year.

Any advice to someone contemplating converting a barn? Expect the worse – it almost certainly happens! You will probably spend a lot more than you bargained, so just accept the fact that converting is going to be more expensive than building on a green-field site. There can be a lot of work that needs to be done by hand and that costs.

Spend plenty of time at the design stage – it's critical. There is never an obvious way of converting a building, or if there is, it is not always the best. You see so many conversions that are dog's dinners, which is a shame. Spend time exploring different options and ideas and you will end up with something that's really attractive and makes the best of the building. Having the right architect is essential.

Finally you need to be the sort of person who is comfortable making compromises about how you are going to live in the building. If you insist on all the features you would find in a modern house, you are not going to be satisfied with a barn. Its construction will stop you from doing that. If you try to shoe-horn 21st-century living into a 19th-century envelope, you will make some awful mistakes.

A spacious garden and a beautiful view may be part of the reason for moving to the country.

CHAPTER EIGHT

Maintenance and repairs

Maintenance is important to buildings of all ages and types. The message to homeowners is simple: prevention is better than cure. By spotting and dealing with problems promptly, you save both time and money in the long run. A few pounds spent fixing a leaky gutter can save hundreds that you might be forced to spend on more substantial repairs if that leak is ignored.

Regular checks are a vital part of building maintenance and there are several that you should carry out frequently to ensure your house is watertight and well cared for. Use binoculars to look for slipped slates and tiles every month and check roofspace every six months, particularly after heavy rain. In addition, aim to carry out a more thorough inspection once a year, from the top of the building to its toes. Think of your home as you do your car. You service your car annually to keep it running smoothly – do the same for your home.

The importance of keeping up appearances

Restoring a wreck or redecorating a newly purchased home is exciting and rewarding work. You see dramatic results and can feel pride in what you have achieved. Maintenance, by contrast, can seem depressingly mundane. By definition, it is never 'done', as new jobs are constantly cropping up and many need tackling surprisingly regularly. Replacing roof tiles or clearing gutters are tasks that can seem unduly repetitious, with the satisfaction of seeing neat and tidy results lasting only a few months. So why bother?

There are plenty of good reasons why regular maintenance is worthwhile. A well-taken-care-of property will almost always retain its value, which means when you come to sell it, all that regular work will have more than paid for itself.

Keeping on top of small jobs also makes your home more enjoyable to live in. It's far more pleasant to live in a house that doesn't have creeping mould on its walls, leaking gutters or peeling wallpaper. You can also rest easy at night knowing that your property is safe. Damp or leaks are not only inconvenient but dangerous, particularly in a property with elderly gas or electrical installations.

As is often the case in life, if you ignore a problem, it doesn't go away, it gets bigger. The same is true of houses; spend a little time regularly maintaining your home and this limits the need for extensive repairs later. It is far easier to check gutters and drains

twice a year for blockages than to cope with a major outbreak of dry rot in roof trusses caused by years of neglect.

If you own an old building, you also have a responsibility to maintain it. Old buildings are a monument to skill and hard work. All the effort and materials that it took to construct them will be wasted if they are allowed to decay. As the owner of an old building, it is your responsibility to preserve and protect it, both out of respect for the past and so that future generations can enjoy it. Well-looked-after old buildings enrich our quality of life. They help preserve a sense of place at a time when familiar neighbourhoods are often under pressure to change and modernise. They foster a sense of continuity with our past and are also a legacy to pass on to our children. If they are to have something worthwhile to inherit, we must look after our old and traditionally built structures now.

How to inspect your home

In order to spot what maintenance jobs need doing and where repairs are necessary, it is a good idea to carry out a thorough inspection of your home at least once a year. Keeping an eye out for early warning signs of decay means you can take prompt remedial action. Some parts of your home need checking even more frequently; the list below details what to look for and how often. Ideally, do the inspection when it is raining – that way you will be able to tell quickly if gutters are blocked or the roof is leaking.

First, it is useful to understand the four key causes of decay in a building. These are: (1) the weather (especially when it results in damp, the main enemy of buildings); (2) fungi, plants and animals; (3) human factors; (4) fires and flood. Every building is affected differently by these factors, but they all suffer from some of them to an extent.

To safeguard your home, begin by simply cleaning leaves and debris from gutters and downpipes, particularly after autumn's leaf fall; similarly, unblock air bricks that ventilate the area beneath a timber floor by clearing away leaves and rubbish. Dampness caused by blocked or leaking gutters and poor ventilation promotes fungal and insect attack in a property. To minimise fire risk, get chimneys swept regularly and ensure that any empty areas or little nooks in the building – for example, loft space or space behind cupboards – are kept clear of rubbish, which can attract vermin that may then gnaw through electrical cabling.

If your property is large, you may need to employ a professional to carry out an inspection. A reputable builder can carry out a basic examination to alert you to any problems. If you use a registered company belonging to a major trade association, it is less likely to recommend unnecessary work.

A structural engineer or specialist building surveyor can also carry out an inspection. He or she will produce a report that recommends repairs in order of priority and can oversee the work. Always choose an independent, objective adviser and one well experienced in working on old buildings. Many building professionals are only familiar with modern construction methods and are not sufficiently qualified to deal with an old building. They may not know what they are looking for and could recommend inappropriate repairs or be unaware of cost-effective solutions.

Carrying out your own inspection

If your property is small, you can do the inspection yourself. First, put together a file with the results of any previous inspections, including areas you need to check again. Add to this any research you have done into your home's history (see chapter six), which will help you understand its important features, the materials used and the way it was put together.

Kit yourself out in the right gear and with proper equipment. You will need to wear overalls and carry a notepad and pencil, a powerful torch, binoculars for inspecting out of the way corners and high-level areas, a pocket knife, a small mirror for looking up or behind narrow openings and a magnet for identifying iron and steel. Take a camera, too, so you can photograph areas that you might want to discuss with a specialist later. Draw up a checklist of all the key elements of the building's construction, detailed below, and investigate each one methodically and thoroughly. Carry out some basic maintenance work as you go along: unblocking gutters and checking that rainwater is flowing through downpipes correctly, for example.

Start at the roof and work downwards, then come inside and, starting in the roof space, work down floor by floor. Remember to look in hidden spaces like cupboards. Check all the pipework for leaks and inspect internal and external

woodwork by poking it with a pocket knife. Do this on floorboards, beams, windowsills and frames. Wood that is very soft may have rot that needs treating, or indicate that the roof is leaking. Note down any fungal or insect infestation and record the condition of all paintwork.

Some faults will be historic and of no further risk – for example, signs of woodworm in floorboards that simply indicate an attack in the past but do not mean the boards are unsound or still infested. Some faults will be minor and will need addressing soon but not urgently, and some will be more serious.

If you find a problem that you do not know how to tackle, consult a professional. A surveyor, architect or structural engineer will be able to offer independent advice. Find one who specialises in old buildings and their repair. An independent specialist has nothing to sell you but his advice and will steer you away from people who want to sell you treatments you do not need. If you go straight to a remedial treatment company, they have a vested interest in selling you their products and you may end up with a quote for unnecessary repairs or inappropriate work.

Once you have carried out the inspection and spoken to any professionals, you can decide which jobs need tackling immediately and which can wait, to be dealt with when there is enough similar work to warrant the expenditure.

A word on safety…

Be aware of safety issues when carrying out maintenance work. Ladders, lofts and roofs are the major hazards, so watch where you tread, especially in roof spaces, and always have enough light to work by. It's best not to work alone, either, but don't forget to take into account the safety of anyone working with you.

You will need safety equipment for some jobs, even if they seem simple. Wear gloves and goggles when cleaning out gutters, especially if you are reaching up from below when debris can easily fall into your eyes. Ensure ladders are securely positioned and strong. If you have any doubts about safe access, particularly on roofs, use a builder, who may need to erect scaffolding if access is not possible with a ladder.

When it comes to electricity, never touch old cabling. Always consult a qualified,

experienced electrician who can first determine its condition. The same goes for oil and gas installations. They can be dangerous if mishandled.

Finding out more

The Society for the Protection of Ancient Buildings (SPAB) sells a range of useful books about building maintenance and also publishes inexpensive guides to specific aspects of building repair. Each November it organises National Maintenance Week, with talks, events and advice on maintaining your home.

Good public libraries will also have copies of these books or can order them for you. The British Standards Institution (BSI) and the Building Research Establishment (BRE) also publish useful titles. If you have a listed building, the English Heritage publication *The Repair of Historic Buildings: Advice on Principles and Methods* is very informative. It also publishes free guidance leaflets on selected topics. You should also contact your local planning authority: many issue guidance on repair techniques and local methods. On the internet, have a look at the Institute of Historic Building Conservation site (www.ihbc.org.uk) or www.buildingconservation.com. Both are useful databases.

Key areas to check

Before you carry out your inspection, draw up a checklist of the key areas that may need attention from the list below. If you find serious problems that need repair or specialist help, there's information on how to go about that and who to contact. Remember that in some cases maintenance work may require permission, such as listed building consent. Current legislation also prevents disturbance of certain types of flora, fauna and wildlife, including bats, many types of orchid and rare thistles and ferns.

Roofs in general

Keeping your home watertight is essential, so check your roof regularly. A builder or surveyor with the necessary safety equipment is best equipped to carry out a detailed roof inspection, but a neighbouring property can be a useful vantage point and binoculars can help. Broken slates and tiles on the ground are a clue that there may be a problem. If slates and tiles are dislodged or missing, have replacements reinstated before damage occurs to the roof timbers or plaster ceilings.

Use a brush to clear moss off roofs: it can block gutters and retain moisture, which may damage the roof covering in frosty weather. Again, you may need a builder to do this since access and safety are issues.

Check:
- Slipped tiles and slates every month
- Roof spaces, especially during rainy weather, every six months
- Moss growth annually

Slate roofs

Look out for moss and ivy, as both can harm a slate roof. Moss can harbour damp, which causes slate to deteriorate, while ivy growing over slate tiles can crack them. Moss-removing washes are available, while ivy can be controlled by simply cutting it back. If the ivy has spread right across the roof, cut the stem at the base and allow the plant to wither before pulling it off.

Use binoculars to see if any slates have slipped or are missing. Generally, the supporting timbers and fixings deteriorate before the slate does and the tiles can loosen. If you need to replace slates or repair damage, always use a specialist local roofing contractor because materials and traditions vary from place to place. The SPAB can advise on suitable contractors.

Check:
- Slipped tiles and slates every month
- Moss growth annually

The roof on an old rural property needs regular inspection.

Clay-tiled roofs

The same advice for slate tiles (see above) applies to clay tiles. If you need to replace old clay tiles, seek out a specialist company that produces tiles using traditional methods and local materials, to ensure you get a good match (see chapter nine). Simply send off a sample, or even just a photograph, of your roof's tiles. Remember that new replacement tiles should match the colour of the originals when they were first laid, not as they look today. In a few years they will weather and blend in. Expect to pay around 85p (plus VAT) for a handmade roof tile.

Check:
- Slipped tiles and slates every month
- Moss growth annually

Thatch

Moss growing in thatch damages its performance and spoils its appearance. If you are worried about the amount growing over your roof, get advice from a professional thatcher rather than trying to rip it out yourself, which could harm the thatch. Check that wire netting installed to stop birds and vermin stealing the thatch for nests is still in good condition. To minimise the risk of fire, make sure the roof space is free from dust and debris and carefully inspect the chimney stack for small holes. These let hot gases into the thatch that could ignite it. It's a good idea to fit a smoke alarm in the roof space.

Check:
- Roof space and chimney stack every six months
- Moss growth annually

External joinery

Wooden doors and windowsills take a greater beating from the elements than any other form of joinery, so they tend to deteriorate more quickly, even when made of hardwood. Check whether paintwork is cracked or flaking and in need of a fresh coat. Softwood joinery exposed to the weather needs a protective coat of paint more often than internal woodwork – aim to do it every three to five years.

Look out for cracks or open joints – these should be filled to prevent water from seeping in, leading to rot or decay. Missing putty around glass should also be replaced, or water may rot the glazing bars. Make sure your gutters and downpipes are not leaking – this can lead to wet rot in the joinery.

Check:
- Paintwork annually
- Condition of wood annually

Rainwater disposal systems

Clear plants, leaves and muck out of gutters and drainage channels every spring and autumn. If your house is surrounded by trees or is a popular perch for pigeons, you may need to do this more often. In wet weather, look for blocked downpipes. When it's dry, look for stained, wet brickwork that may indicate a leaking pipe. Clear away any plants growing behind downpipes, as they can force them off the wall and crack them. Use a mirror to look behind old cast-iron pipes for splits. They often occur here and are tricky to spot. If gutters are sloping and spilling rainwater against the house walls, you will need to get them refitted. Check the quality of paintwork on any cast-iron pipes and gutters: regular repainting is necessary to prevent rust. Clean out gulleys beneath rainwater pipes by hand (wearing gloves).

Check:
- Obvious leaks or blockages monthly
- Downpipes and gutters in heavy rain every six months

Brick walls

Bricks can last for centuries as long as the mortar between them is in good condition, so check that the pointing is not decayed. If it deteriorates, rainwater can penetrate the masonry, causing the bricks to flake and leading to damp and rot.

Badly eroded mortar joints should be repointed. If your house predates 1900, you will have to use lime and sand mix, rather than modern cement, to do this. Although many builders will be quick to suggest repointing, sometimes it is best to do nothing and just leave the brickwork alone, provided you have first fixed the cause of the problem, such as water leaking into the brickwork from a damaged downpipe.

When necessary, some form of conservative repair can be done: brickwork needs to be taken down and rebuilt only in exceptional circumstances. Only bricks that are severely damaged should be cut out and replaced. Getting an exact replica is difficult, but there are a number of good suppliers producing new handmade bricks at reasonable prices (typically about £1 a brick). Replacement bricks should match the existing ones as closely as possible in size, colour, texture and durability and should be laid in the same way using the same type of bond or pattern.

You can also buy bricks from salvage yards, but finding a good match can be difficult and quality is variable. Older bricks may be damaged or have aged badly and, if you are buying a large consignment, you cannot be sure how many defective bricks are included in your bulk order.

Check:
- Pointing annually

Stone

Stone is a durable material; its main problem is discolouration. Pale stonework exposed to pollution can become darker. If you are concerned about this, talk to your local conservation officer. Most authorities and associations advise against cleaning stone unless absolutely necessary – for example, where a wall has graffiti. Cleaning methods can be harsh, involving sandblasting or powerful chemicals that rob the stone of its mellow patina. Natural weathering simply reflects the history of a building and isn't something to worry about.

Check:

- Condition of stonework annually (although prompt cleaning of graffiti is recommended to deter copycat incidents)

Render

Look out for cracks in render that can let in rainwater. In winter, cracks combined with frost can cause render to fall off. Tap around any cracks to work out how much render is loose – a hollow sound tells you it is. Missing areas can be patched – traditional lime render is readily available.

Check:

- Cracks in render every six months

Ironwork

Flaking paintwork lets water in and causes rust. Where ironwork has corroded extensively, it can be sandblasted or flame cleaned – a job for the professionals – before priming and repainting.

It is common to find sections of wrought iron that have broken, but often they can be welded back together. If you need to replace exterior ironwork, plenty of companies can make railings and balconies to traditional designs, or simply contact your local blacksmith and talk through your needs. If existing original elements can be dismantled and transported, a replica can be cast from these to get a faithful match.

Check:

- Paintwork and rust annually

Ceilings

Look out for signs of water damage. Damp patches or stains indicate a leak in the walls or roof that needs fixing. Keep an eye out for cracks, too. Cracks do not necessarily mean the ceiling needs replacing: a skilled plasterer can patch them up and reattach cornices and mouldings fairly easily. Note how many cracks there are, though. If they increase each month or so, it may be a sign of problems with the roof structure or movement in the building.

Check:

- Water damage and cracks every six months

Internal joinery

Check for signs of rot in enclosed areas, under stairs or in cupboards. If you find rot, treat the underlying cause – usually poor ventilation or damp. Be wary of using remedial treatment companies who may recommend more work than is necessary.

Check that you can open and close doors easily, without forcing them, which damages the door and frame. Doors often stick because of badly fitted hinges, which can be easily repaired. If stair rails or balustrades are loose, get them repaired or replaced – a wood turner will be able to make a good replica.

If internal joinery is damaged, replace only what is necessary and retain as much of the original as you can. An experienced joiner can use a technique called piecing in, which adds matching timber to the existing to repair it. It's straightforward work to a skilled joiner and helps save the old parts of the building while also producing an effective repair.

Do not assume the worst. Problems like warped doors and loose joints can be rectified by a joiner, while joinery affected by fungal rot or insect attack may not need to be removed, provided the leak or damp that first caused it has been fixed.

Check:
- Decay in timber annually

Subsidence

Subsidence occurs in houses built on clay or with large trees growing nearby whose roots can shift the foundations. Look out for diagonal cracks greater than 5mm wide in the walls. Check them monthly to establish whether they are increasing in length and width, which would indicate that there is on-going structural movement. If a crack appears minor, repointing with an appropriate mortar will prevent moisture from entering. If the crack opens further after pointing, seek the advice of a structural engineer.

Check:
- Minor cracks and new cracks annually
- Diagonal cracks more than 5mm wide monthly

Damp

As with rot, always aim to treat the cause rather than symptoms. If you need help, consult a surveyor for independent advice (remedial companies have a vested interest in their own recommendations).

Check:
- Signs of damp every six months

CHAPTER NINE

Directory

This section contains a number of invaluable resources for anyone buying or working on their own country property. The Directory provides the starting point for buying a property, finding the right builders, surveyors and other professional bodies and choosing the best craftspeople in your area. Most companies have a website which means that a lot of the research can be done from home.

House finding and buying services

1stlocate 0113 228 4452; www.1stlocate.co.uk; in Scotland www.housepricescotland.com.

Association of Relocation Agents 08700 737475; www.relocationagents.com. The professional body for the UK relocation industry.

Buildstore 0870 870 9991; www.buildstore.co.uk. Self-build and renovation advice, products and services.

Charcol 0800 358 5885; http://mortgages.charcolonline.co.uk. Mortgage advisors and brokers.

Church of Scotland Law Department 0131 225 5722; www.cofsproperties.org.uk.

Council of Mortgage Lenders 020 7437 0075; www.cml.org.uk. Trade association for mortgage lenders in Britain, promoting good lending practice.

Ecology Building Society 0845 674 5566; www.ecology.co.uk.

Estate Angels www.estateangels.co.uk. Free service that emails all of your chosen estate agents with your details in one go. Estate agents then contact you with property details.

Land Registry 020 7917 8888; www.landreg.gov.uk.

Neighbourhood Statistics www.neighbourhood.statistics.gov.uk. Government site where you can view, compare or download statistics for local areas on a wide range of subjects including population, crime, health and housing.

Norwich and Peterborough Building Society 01733 372372; www.npbs.co.uk.

Pavilions of Splendour 020 8348 1234; www.heritage.co.uk.

Period Property UK 07000 312640; www.periodproperty.co.uk. Properties for sale plus other information.

The Property Organisation 01892 813985; www.property.org.uk.

Rightmove www.rightmove.co.uk. Online estate agency.

SAVE 020 7253 3500; www.savebritainsheritage.org.

Stags www.stags.co.uk. Estate agency based in the southwest.

Strutt & Parker 020 7629 7282; www.struttandparker.co.uk. Nationwide estate agents.

Insurance services

Chubb Insurance www.chubb.com. Insurers specialising in wrecks under renovation.

County Insurance Services 01865 842084; www.county-insurance.co.uk. Specialist insurance, including thatched homes.

Hiscox 0845 330 9505; www.hiscox.com. Insurers specialising in wrecks under renovation.

NFU Mutual 0800 316 4661; www.nfumutual.co.uk. Specialist insurance, including thatched homes.

Builders, architects, surveyors

Architects Accredited in Building Conservation 01625 871458; www.aabc-register.co.uk.

The Association for Environment Conscious Building www.aecb.net. Independent environmental building trade organisation with network of members and publications.

Federation of Master Builders 020 7242 7583; www.fmb.org.uk.

Heritage Building Contractors Group 01543 414234; www.buildingconservation.com.

Institution of Civil Engineers 020 7222 7722; www.ice.org.uk.

Joint Contracts Tribunal www.jctltd.co.uk. Publishes contracts for the construction industry, available through RIBA, RICS and CIP Limited (Construction Industry Publications).

Office of the Deputy Prime Minister www.odpm.gov.uk. Useful information about planning permission, building regulations and party wall act.

Royal Incorporation of Architects in Scotland 0131 229 7545; www.rias.org.uk.

Royal Institute of British Architects (RIBA) 020 7307 3700; www.riba.org.

Professional bodies and advice sources

Royal Institute of Structural Engineers (RISE) 020 7235 4535; www.istructe.org.uk.

Royal Institution of Chartered Surveyors (RICS) 0870 333 1600; www.rics.org. For information on auction houses and auctioneers, look at www.rics.org/property_auctions.

UK Network of Building Surveyors and Structural Engineers 0800 525850; www.surveyorsreports.co.uk. Nationwide network of surveyors, engineers etc.

The Architectural Heritage Fund 020 7925 0199; www.ahfund.org.uk. Registered charity promoting the conservation of historic buildings in Britain. Advice, information, grants and low interest loans for projects undertaken by building preservation trusts (BPTs) and other charities.

British Standards Institution (BSI) 020 8996 9001; www.bsi-global.com.

The Building Centre 020 7692 4000; www.buildingcentre.co.uk. Extensive library with information on building and home improvement, including products and materials, standards and codes of practice.

The Building Conservation Directory 01747 871717; www.buildingconservation.com. Source for finding specialist products and services.

Building Research Establishment (BRE) 01923 664000; www.bre.co.uk.

CADW: Welsh Historic Monuments 029 2050 0200; www.cadw.wales.gov.uk.

Calor Gas 0800 626626; www.calorcountryliving.co.uk.

Carter Jonas 01865 404423;
www.carterjonas.co.uk. Building
consultancy, planning and development,
listed building conservation and
restoration. If you are planning to convert a
barn, it has a barns section that can offer a
total package of a site visit by a planner to
advise on viability and value and in-house
surveyors who can draw up plans for the
work.

Centre for Sustainable Energy
0117 929 9950; free advice line 0117 929
9404; www.cse.org.uk.

Clear Skies 0870 243 0930;
www.clearskies.gov.uk. Government
initiative offering grants for
environmentally friendly domestic
installations.

**The Crown Guild of Master
Woodcarvers** 01278 424246;
www.woodcarversguild.com. Master
woodcarvers, furniture and architectural
fitting makers guild. Find a craftsman, buy
direct from workshops or commission a
bespoke piece.

**Department for the Environment, Food
and Rural Affairs** (DEFRA) 08459
335577; www.defra.gov.uk.

English Heritage 0870 333 1181;
www.english-heritage.org.uk.

English Nature 01733 455000;
www.english-nature.org.uk.

Environment Agency 08708 506506;
www.environment-agency.gov.uk. The
website has a flood map where you can
pinpoint areas at risk from flooding.

**Environment and Heritage Service
Northern Ireland** 028 9054 3034;
www.ehsni.gov.uk.

The Georgian Group 020 7529 8920;
www.georgiangroup.org.uk.

The Green Building Press
01559 370908; www.newbuilder.co.uk.
Publishes *The Green Building Bible*
annually, which is packed with information
about ideas and materials.

Heritage Information 020 7637 7744;
www.heritageinformation.org.uk.

Historic Scotland www.historic-
scotland.gov.uk. Repair grants,
conservation bureau, advice and more.

The House Historians 0117 932 3009;
www.thehousehistorians.co.uk.

**The Institute of Historic Building
Conservation** 01747 873133;
www.ihbc.org.uk.

Law Society of Scotland
0131 226 7411; www.lawscot.org.uk.

Listed Property Owners Club
01795 844939; www.lpoc.co.uk.
Information and advice to owners of listed
property, including guidance on grants,
specialist property insurance and practical
maintenance advice.

**The National Inspection Council for
Electrical Installation Contracting**
(NICEIC) 020 7564 2320 (technical
helpline); www.niceic.org.uk. List of
approved electricians plus information.

Oil Firing Technical Association (Oftec)
0901 4700 112 (technical helpline);
www.oftec.org.

Period Property UK
www.periodproperty.co.uk. Specialist
advice, a renovating section, books, a
discussion forum and a property buying
and selling area.

**Scottish Society for Conservation and
Restoration** (SSCR) 01506 811777;
www.sscr.demon.co.uk.

**Society for the Protection
of Ancient Buildings** (SPAB)
020 7377 1644; www.spab.org.uk. Advice,
books, leaflets, practical courses, lectures
and campaigning.

Thatching Advisory Services
01264 773820;
www.thatchingadvisoryservices.co.uk.

**United Kingdom Institute
for Conservation** (UKIC)
020 7721 8721; www.ukic.org.uk and
www.conservationregister.com.
Publications, training courses, information
and special events. Register of specialist
conservation companies and craftspeople.

The Victorian Society 020 8994 1019;
www.victorian-society.org.uk. Information
and advice source for owners of Victorian
property.

Courses

The Lime Centre 01962 713636;
www.thelimecentre.co.uk. Practical one-day
courses on lime and its uses.

**Society for the Protection of Ancient
Buildings** (SPAB) see above.

**University of York Centre for
Conservation** 01904 433901;
www.york.ac.uk/depts/arch.

**Weald and Downland Open
Air Museum** 01243 811464;
www.wealddown.co.uk. Centre of
excellence in building conservation with a
variety of courses throughout the year.

West Dean College 01243 811301;
www.westdean.org.uk. Graduate and
postgraduate diplomas in conservation and
restoration of buildings interiors and sites.

Specialist suppliers and craftspeople

Bulmer Brick & Tile Co 01787 269232.
Hand- and custom-made bricks to match
any period, from Roman times onwards.
Part or whole arches, plus restoration of
brick floors.

Calch Ty-Mawr Lime 01874 658249;
www.lime.org.uk. Welsh centre for
traditional and ecological building. Lime
products, paints, building materials, tools
and books, plus advice, courses and site
visits.

Chris Topp & Co 01845 501415;
www.christopp.co.uk. Restoration of
ancient ironwork, casting design,
mouldings and window frames and general
blacksmithing in cast iron, wrought iron,
brass, bronze, copper and steel.

Cole & Son 020 8442 8844;
www.cole-and-son.com. Hand-block,
screen-print and surface-printed wallpapers
with a huge patterns archive.

GP & J Baker 020 7351 7760;
www.gpjbaker.co.uk. Fabric and wallpaper
designs based on historical archives.

Holkham Linseed Paints
01328 711348;
www.holkhamlinseedpaints.co.uk.
Long-lasting oil and emulsion paint using
natural sustainable linseed oil made on the
Holkham Estate in Norfolk. Plus courses

Heating and lighting

on how to use the paints and on window restoration.

Mike Wye & Associates
01409 281644; www.mikewye.co.uk. Lime products, natural paints, insulation, laths, lintels, reed mats. Plus practical one-day courses.

Natural Building Technologies 01844 338338; www.natural-building.co.uk. Natural paints, insulation, lime, earth and timber products.

The Old House Store 0118 969 6949; www.oldhousestore.co.uk. For traditional and ecological materials, plus courses in building conservation, including pointing and plastering with lime.

The Real Paint and Varnish Co 01539 623662; www.realpaints.com. Large range of lead paints for restoration of grade I and II* listed buildings.

Salvo 01890 820499; www.salvo.co.uk. Directory of salvage yards, dealers and restorers around Britain that subscribe to the Salvo code, plus items for sale or wanted.

Thermafleece 01768 486285; www.secondnatureuk.com. Insulation made from British sheep's wool.

Agas and Rayburns Order a brochure online at www.aga-rayburn.co.uk.

Foundation Firewood 01763 271271; www.fbc.demon.co.uk. Distributors of environmentally friendly Baxi wood boilers in Britain.

Just Generators 01263 820202; www.justgenerators.co.uk.

The Organic Energy Company 0845 458 4076; www.organicenergy.co.uk. Wood-pellet stoves and boilers plus pellet suppliers.

Index

Picture credits

Adrian Briscoe pages 105, 136
Charlie Colmer pages 6, 22, 63, 107, 124, 135, 143
Erin Hadyn O'Neill page 123
Andrea Jones pages 88–89
James Merrell pages 90
Diana Miller pages 67, 100
Clay Perry page 25
Alex Ramsey pages 33, 40
Pippa Rimmer pages 26, 54, 108
Kim Sayer pages 13, 83, 97 (right)
William Shaw 2, 76, 95, 97 (left), 39, 45, 48, 129, 148
Bob Smith page 50
Peter Woloszynski pages 44, 115

Jacket front Charlie Colmer